NEW TESTAMENT
CHURCH PRINCIPLES

NEW TESTAMENT CHURCH PRINCIPLES

by

ARTHUR G. CLARKE

Author of *Analytical Studies in the Psalms*
and other works.

JOHN RITCHIE LTD
CHRISTIAN PUBLICATIONS

40 Beansburn, Kilmarnock, Scotland

ISBN - 13: 978 0 946351 11 4
ISBN - 10: 0 946351 11 2

Copyright © 2009 by John Ritchie Ltd.
40 Beansburn, Kilmarnock, Scotland

www.ritchiechristianmedia.co.uk

Typeset by John Ritchie Ltd., Kilmarnock
Printed by Bell & Bain

EXTRACT FROM PREFACE
TO THE FIRST EDITION

The following chapters are based upon mimeographed notes of lectures given by the author to a weekly class of Bible students in Bermuda. The notes first appeared in print as a series of articles in the magazine *Precious Seed,* the editor of which, in a short word of explanation to readers, mentions that the terse style of the original was retained so that much ground could be covered in a minimum space. The same reason applies to the set-up of the present booklet. Moreover, as a convenient little handbook quick reference is thereby facilitated. All Scripture passages indicated should be diligently turned to and prayerfully considered in the spirit of the Bereans (Acts 17.10-11). It is hardly to be expected that all will agree with the interpretations given under the headings of "Misunderstood Texts" (pp. 25 & 94). In a class of keen Bible students, however, it is not wise to bypass difficult Scriptures. Sooner or later they will probably be brought forward at question time. Greater confidence is promoted if the leader will state his views with conviction but without dogmatism.

The author owes an immense debt of gratitude to highly esteemed servants of Christ of this and former generations, whose oral and written teachings under God have contributed so much to a better understanding of His Word on these important themes.

December 1955   ARTHUR G. CLARKE

PREFACE TO THE SECOND EDITION

That another edition should be called for within so few months is a matter for praise to God, for it surely betokens a measure of revived interest in the truths of which the booklet treats. May the Holy Spirit further stimulate God's children to follow divine precepts and patterns rather than descend to human expedients.

A few minor corrections have now been made, but in the main the text remains unchanged.

June 1956   A. G. C.

PREFACE TO THE THIRD EDITION

Because of continued requests for copies since the second edition was exhausted many months ago, this third edition is now put forth in the hope that it, too, will find ready acceptance among the saints. At the suggestion of several esteemed and experienced brethren on both sides of the Atlantic and to whom I owe sincere thanks, the little book appears in a new format. It has been carefully revised and rewritten with the text somewhat extended to give greater facility in reading. In its new form with larger type and improved covers the book should prove more useful as a work of reference.

October 1961   A. G. C.

PREFACE TO THE FOURTH EDITION

The issue of this further English edition is welcomed as requests for copies of the work continue to be received. Since it was first published it has been translated into several languages including African dialects, Chinese and Hindi. Its appeal, especially to translators, has been both its comprehensiveness and its conciseness. Little did the writer think when he first prepared these notes for lectures to Bible students in Bermuda well over twenty years ago that they would be found useful to God's people in so many parts of the world.

In these days of increasing departure from the faith once for all delivered to the saints (Jude v.3, RV) and the frequent introduction of practices contrary to scriptural church order, there is a pressing need to re-affirm the principles which our Lord Jesus Christ as Head of His church universal would have the locally gathered companies of believers represent and serve Him in a hostile world.

May 1975   A. G. C.

LIST OF ABBREVIATIONS

CONTENTS

FOREWORD

It gives me much pleasure to write a foreword commending the Bible Notes written by Mr. A. G. Clarke on certain basic doctrines of the New Testament. I have read them with profit and hope they will have a wide circulation. If the members of the local assemblies are to be built up in the faith once for all delivered to the saints, it is necessary that they be instructed in the principles declared by the Apostles in their letters to the churches. There is a sad tendency today to lessen interest in doctrine, but it is essential to know the mind of the Lord as revealed in the Scriptures concerning the Christian's life, walk, fellowship and service. Only so can the children of God be established and maintain an effective witness.

The notes as now issued provide an intelligent starting-point in the study of the Word, and it is hoped that by diligent reading of the indicated Scriptures and application of the Truth, young Christians especially will be helped to a fuller and more useful service for God, growing both in grace and in knowledge of our Lord Jesus Christ.

G. J. HYDE.

ACKNOWLEDGMENT
by the Editor of *Precious Seed*

Grateful memories of help and encouragement received when a young believer from Mr. A. G. Clarke ensures that anything from his pen is of interest to me. When it was learned that notes of lectures given in Bermuda had been preserved I was eager to read them. On doing so it became immediately apparent that here was a most valuable re-statement of Scripture teaching regarding the local church. My next impression was of the enormous amount of preparatory work entailed in compressing so comprehensive, sane and balanced a presentation of the truth in such comparatively small compass. Whilst, no doubt, the appreciation and profit of the students for whom the lectures were designed justified the amount of conscientious labour involved, it was felt that the Notes not only deserved but would meet a cordial reception in a more extensive field. We were accordingly glad to have permission to reproduce them in *Precious Seed,* a bi-monthly magazine for promoting the study of scriptural church principles. The enthusiastic welcome received from our readers amply confirmed our conviction. The Notes have already proved particularly helpful to keen young Christians eager for a plain and concise treatment of this wide subject. It is gratifying to learn that they will now be available in more permanent form, for we are confident that with God's continued blessing they will remain a means of edification for a long while to come. As the Notes are intended to induce study, we are sure the author has done well to retain the terse style.

JAMES H. LARGE

CHAPTER ONE

THE CHURCH AND THE CHURCHES

INTRODUCTION. During the course of our Lord's earthly ministry, He had occasion to charge the Pharisees and Scribes with nullifying the word of God by their traditions. Said He, "Ye leave the commandment of God and hold fast the tradition of men", and cited the prophecy of Isaiah, "This people honoureth me with their lips but their heart is far from me. But in vain do they worship me, teaching as their doctrines the precepts of men" (Mk 7.6-13; Mt 15.3-9, RV). In Christendom today a similar pernicious state of affairs is to be found. Early departure from the simplicity of the gospel has resulted in the great confusion of doctrine and practice observable among the many divisions of the Christian Church.

In applying ourselves to the study of the present subject, it is necessary, therefore, to emphasize that the word of God must be our only authority. It is an all-sufficient guide for the people of God (2 Tim 3.16-17), ever bearing in mind the fact that the indwelling Holy Spirit affords His gracious help (1 Jn 2.20). All doctrine and practice should be tested by the authoritative "Thus saith the Lord".

DEFINITION. Let us consider the definition of the word "church". There are two popular misconceptions. The first is that "church" refers to a material building, whether consecrated or not, erected for the holding of religious services by a Christian community. The second misconception is that "church" refers to an organised society of professed Christians bearing some distinctive name or governed by an ordained form of control. These are ideas quite foreign to God's Word. For the true meaning we note that the Greek word *ecclesia,* which is translated "church", literally signifies an "outcalling", a called-out company of people, an assembly. It is used in the New Testament of Israel (Acts 7.38); of an Ephesian mob (19.32); of the regular legal assembly at Ephesus (19.39); and, finally, of the Church of God as a body of persons called out in separation from the world. The first occurrence of the word in this last sense is in Matthew 16.18.

COMPOSITION. What constitutes "the Church" and "a church"? The answer is that the former is universal, the latter local.

1. The Universal Church is composed solely of true believers on the Lord Jesus Christ, the Son of God. They are persons "born anew", "born from above" (Jn 3.3, RV & RVm) by the Holy Spirit of God and forming the invisible, indivisible and inviolable company of the redeemed in this present age. Relative to the Church's *origination* refer to Ephesians 3.3-12; Colossians 1.24-27. For its *inauguration,* see Matthew 16.18; Acts 2. This was consequent upon Christ's finished work on the Cross, His resurrection and ascension, and coincident with the personal descent of the Holy Spirit at Pentecost.

Its *completion* will be at the personal descent of the Lord Jesus to the air (1 Thess 4.13-18).

2. The Local Church is composed of a company of professed believers in any locality and gathering in the name of Christ (Mt 18.20, the simplest form) and owning a three-fold authority, namely, the headship of the Lord Jesus, the control of the Holy Spirit and the teaching of the Word of God. Only true believers are primarily contemplated (1 Cor 1.2), but unbelievers may creep in (Acts 8.9-13, 18-23; 20.29; 2 Pet 2.1; Jude v.4). Mixed membership of believers and known unbelievers in a church is wholly unscriptural. For the local church aspect turn to Acts 8.1; 13.1; Revelation 2.1,8, etc. For use in the plural see Acts 15.41; 16.5; 1 Corinthians 7.17; Revelation 2.1; 22.16. Such companies are called "churches of God", denoting their origin and ownership (1 Thess 2.14); "churches of Christ", denoting their redemption and responsibility (Rom 16.16); "churches of the saints" denoting their composition and character (1 Cor 14.33); and, lastly, "churches of the Gentiles" denoting their election and extension (Rom 16.4 with Acts 15.3-4; 9.15).

FUNCTION. We will now consider what is the character of the Church and what purpose it serves. These are indicated by various descriptive terms or analogies. Here again it is needful to discriminate between the universal and local aspects.

1. The Universal Church is ever to be viewed in relation to Christ. It is designed of God for the glory of His beloved Son. It was never intended to be an agency for the glorification of an arrogant hierarchy seeking political world power. Men often speak of "the Church" as if it were a separate entity having special authority in the aggregate of denominations. This is another misuse of the word.

Figures of speech found in the New Testament relative to the Church of Christ are very interesting and deeply instructive. They are as follows:

(a) A *Body* (Rom 12.4-5; 1 Cor 12.12-13; Eph 1.22-23; 4.4; Col 1.18). In Ephesians the Body is viewed as the complement of the Head and in Colossians as complete in the Head. A vital unity between Christ the Head and Christians as members of His Body is indicated. As the Head Christ is seat of the Church's life (Eph 1.11-13 - "in whom"); source of the Church's nourishment (Eph 4.16 - "from whom"); supervisor of the Church's activities (Eph 4.15 - "into him"). Through the members of His Body the Head finds expression on earth. They carry out His will. It should be noted that whilst there is unity of the whole there is variety of function in the individual members.

(b) A *Building* (Eph 2.19-22). The Church is viewed as a spiritual edifice, a holy temple, a sanctuary designed of God for His habitation in the Spirit, truly a noble conception of the divine indwelling. The only other occurrence of the Greek word translated "habitation" is in Revelation 18.2, which presents a striking contrast. The architect of this holy temple is God Himself. He is originator of the plan (Eph 1.4,22; 2 Tim 1.9). Christ is the Builder, and the Bed-rock Foundation (Mt 16.18; cp. 1 Cor 3.11). He is the Chief Corner-stone from which the whole edifice takes alignment (Eph 2.20-21; 1 Pet 2.6; Is 28.16), and the Head-stone, which in its primary meaning pointed to the stone at the very summit of a pyramidal structure or a crowning pinnacle (see 1 Pet 2.7; Mk 12.10-11; Acts 4.10-11). These citations from the Old Testament (Ps 118.22-23) lend support to an ancient Jewish tradition regarding the head-stone of Solomon's temple. Turn also to Zechariah 4.7-9 with reference to the second temple which was erected after the Exile. In the spiritual temple believers are "living stones" (1 Pet 2.5). By some expositors, apostles and prophets (New Testament) are likened to the first course of special stones laid upon a rock foundation (Eph 2.20) but it is better, perhaps, to understand "foundation" to refer to the doctrine of Christ proclaimed by these servants of God (1 Cor 3.10-11; Rom 15.20). In the New Testament the figure of a building merges into that which follows.

(c) A House or Household (1 Pet 2.4-10; 4.17; 1 Tim 3.15; Heb 3.6; 10.21; Eph 2.19; Gal 6.10). The basic thoughts here are responsibility and discipline. The Old Testament type is seen in the tabernacle with its priesthood and Levitical service.

(d) A Bride, The expression "Bride of Christ" is not found in scripture, but many see it implied in Ephesians 5.28-32. It is certainly found in several Old Testament types. It presents the thought of consortship in mutual devotion, loving companionship now and hereafter, and as sharing dominion with her Lord when He comes to reign. For the first clear type of this blessed relationship read Genesis 1.26-28; 2.21-24. In this the Church comes before us in its heavenly and eternal character (Rev 19.7; 21.2 and 9). It identifies the Church also with the next figure.

(e) *A City* (Rev 21.2-10). This seems to point to the Church in its coming millennial age and to the new earth in the eternal state. "City" suggests our Lord's administrative centre. In the midst of His glorified Church He exercises universal government.

(f) *A Flock* (Jn 10.16; 21.15-17); contrast the idea of "fold" - 10.1 and 16. Under the old covenant God's people Israel were kept within the boundary walls of the Law. Under the new the "flock" of true believers is kept together by attraction to the shepherd. The late Mr. Harold Barker used to express it succinctly thus: "A fold is a circumference without a centre; a flock has a centre without a circumference". Christ's shepherd care for His own sheep is emphasized. As Chief Shepherd He appoints under-shepherds, who are the elders in each local assembly.

(g) *A New Man* (Eph 2.11-18). In Christ believing Jews and believing Gentiles are no longer separated but are created one. In this new creation are no racial or social distinctions (1 Cor 12.13; Col 3.10-11). The partition "wall" between Jew and Gentile has been broken down and the "enmity" resulting from the Law's decrees annulled. By His atoning death Christ had in view the reconciliation of both to God. All men are now reached through the gospel on equal terms.

2. The Local Church. The use in the New Testament of certain similar terms for both the universal church and a local assembly clearly underlines the truth that in the mind of the Lord the latter is meant to be a local expression of the whole.

(a) *Body* (1 Cor 12.27). An individual assembly, of course, is not "the Body", neither is it, strictly speaking "a body" (as if Christ had many "Bodies") but it is "body-like", that is to say, what is true of the whole Church in this analogy is true of the local assembly. Subjection to the Head is implied but the emphasis is now placed upon the loving unity, mutual affinity and co-ordinated activity of all the members. Read v.21 and, indeed, the whole context.

(b) *Building* (1 Cor 3.9). The figure here has a double significance pointing to both process and product. It is a sacred habitation, a divine sanctuary. Again it is not "the sanctuary" or, strictly speaking "a sanctuary" but the assembly is to be God's sanctuary in character. The dominant thought is that of holiness. The foundation of a properly constituted local assembly is Christ (1 Cor 3.11).

(c) Tillage (1 Cor 3.9). This also includes both process and product in the figure of a cultivated plot of ground. In this concept is opened up a wide range of profitable study. Fruitfulness is suggested as the divine aim in caring for the local church (Col 1.10).

(d) *Virgin* (2 Cor 11.2). The words of Paul "I espoused you" (RV) cannot refer to the universal church. He is unquestionably referring to the church at Corinth, and it was a needed reminder to the carnal believers there. The maintenance of purity and loyalty to the Lord is to be seen in the local assembly as well as in individual believers.

(e) *Flock* (Acts 20.28-29; 1 Pet 5.2-3). The Greek word is *poimnion,* a diminutive of the more general *poimne,* because it applies to the local assembly not to the whole flock belonging to God. It points to the need of unwearying care on the part of the local under-shepherds, the elders.

(f) *Lampstand* (Rev 1-3). Each individual assembly is viewed in its collective responsibility as a light-bearer for the Lord in the spiritual darkness of the locality. Witness by word is perhaps the dominant thought (Phil 2.16).

(g) *Epistle* (2 Cor 3.3). The local assembly bears great responsibility in its corporate capacity to be a witness for Christ by its conduct before the world.

Witness by walk is the dominant thought. Further explanation as to local church relationships seems desirable.

(a) *In relation to the Lord* the main principle is that of *subjection.* The analogies mentioned above bring out various aspects of this. The same truth is taught in Revelation 1-3. The apostle in his vision saw the risen Lord in the midst of the lampstands, symbolizing the seven assemblies. John sees Him moving among them as sole Supervisor of their testimony for Him. Each assembly is responsible to Him and He deals directly with each. Unlike the golden seven-branched lampstand in the tabernacle of old, these light-bearers are separate. This surely teaches us that the only links between individual assemblies are the *one* Lord (Eph 4.5) and the *one* Spirit (Eph 4.4 - symbolized by the oil in all the lamps). The Lord is the controlling Head and the Holy Spirit is the indwelling power for testimony.

(b) *In relation to other assemblies* the thought of *intercommunion* is prominent. There should always be a close and happy fellowship between all. The New Testament records a constant coming and going among them by servants of Christ for the purpose of ministry and by believers on business or social visits to different places.

It is important to understand that there was, and is to be, no federation of churches, whether bearing a distinctive name or not, no limited or exclusive circle of assemblies, no man-made organization of any kind. Moreover, Scripture affords no support for a central authority, such as, "mother church" or ecclesiastical council, no representative committee of control or other form of administrative body. Leaders and certain elders did sometimes gather for the discussion of important problems of doctrine and practice, and recommendations were made but this was very different from a governing organization.

(c) In relation to the world the clear rule is that of *separation.* Already in this chapter it has been explained that the church is a company of "called out" ones, first, by an individual calling (Jn 17.14-16; Rom 8.30); and secondly, by collective constitution as the Church of God, a people for His Name (Acts 20.28; 15.14; Titus 2.14). It has been shown also that the local church is to bear a character corresponding to the whole (1 Cor 12.27; 3.16-17). "Holy" indicates separation unto God from all worldly systems, for the whole world (*kosmos*) lies in the evil one (1 Jn 5.19, RV). This includes the social world, the political world and the religious world, whether pagan or so-called Christian. Mark the clear command in 2 Corinthians 6.14-18.

In the matter of *local church gatherings* it is noteworthy that whilst Israel's daily life and religious exercises under the Law were regulated down to the last detail by plain commandments, a service which "gendered to bondage" (Gal 4.24-25), Christians have the unspeakable privilege of a service of sonship in joyful liberty (Gal 5.1; 4.6-7; 2 Cor 3.17 and contexts). No festival seasons or fast days are enjoined, and no command whatever as to times and places of meeting (Col 2.16-17; Gal 4.8-11; Rom 14.5-7). Nevertheless, we are not left entirely without guidance. This is to be found in the example of the early Christians and recorded in the Scriptures without doubt for our instruction. We find they met for the following purposes:-

(a) *Breaking of Bread* (Acts 2.42; 20.1-7; 1 Cor 11.23-32). This was the primary object of their coming together on the Lord's Day. See pages 29-38.

(b) *Collective Worship.* Although there appears to be no concrete example in the New Testament of a meeting purely for worship, except when connected with other exercises, obviously it cannot be dissociated from the breaking of bread. Worship in the collective sense as well as the individual aspect is manifest in the proper fulfilment of our priestly functions (pp. 39-45). It is helpful to turn to John 4.23-24; 1 Peter 2.5; Hebrews 13.15; 10.19-25 and Acts 2.47.

(c) *United Prayer.* Gatherings for prayer are frequently recorded in the Book of Acts, and we are thereby taught valuable lessons on the importance of assembly prayer meetings. It is sad that a common complaint heard in these days concerns poor attendance at the week-night prayer session. Read Acts 2.42; 4.24-31; 12.5,12.

(d) *Scripture Reading and Ministry* drew the saints together (Acts 2.42; 11.26; 13.1; 15.30- 32; 20.7; 1 Tim 4.13; 1 Cor 14; Col 4.16). Public reading of the Scriptures was needful in days when the Christian communities contained many illiterates. Moreover manuscript copies were comparatively few and expensive. Even today careful public reading of God's word might well accomplish more than much sermonizing! The subject of ministry is dealt with in ch.7.

(e) *Hearing Reports.* The apostles Peter and John returned from an examination before the religious authorities in Jerusalem and reported to "their own company" (Acts 4.23). This had to do with the local testimony. The report stimulated a response of earnest and effectual prayer (vv.24-31). The giving of missionary reports is exemplified in Acts 14.26-28; 15.3-4,12.

(f) *Needed Discipline. This* required assembly action, 1 Cor 5.4. This subject also is considered later; see pages 67-74.

(g) *Social Intercourse* characterized the saints in the early days of the church. The fellowship of "their own company" was constantly sought. In true separation from an ungodly world, and particularly in times of persecution, it is not to be wondered at that the believers felt drawn together by a common experience (Acts 2.46; 4.23, 32; 2 Pet 2.13; Jude v.12). The "love-feast" (*agape*) referred to was principally a social meal in which there was no distinction of race or class. The holy practice of Christian social intercourse is too often neglected in our days, and this lack is detrimental to a happier fellowship. Brief contacts at church gatherings, with hand-shaking among special friends is considered by not a few to exhaust the social duties of Christians. "Tea-meetings" fulfil useful purposes but do not cover all obligations. The opening of private homes, especially to lonely believers, is a worthwhile service for the Lord. Young converts with an unsympathetic home atmosphere are usually much helped in their testimony by hospitality shown them by devoted Christian families.

CHAPTER TWO

BAPTISM

The Lord Jesus appointed two ordinances only for His Church, namely, Baptism and the Lord's Supper. The Church of Rome has added five others without the least warrant from the Holy Scriptures. They are Confirmation, Penance, Extreme Unction, Holy Orders and Matrimony. We do observe the last, not because it is specifically of the Church order, but because it belongs to the creation order (Gen 2.24). Rome, however, refuses to recognise marriage outside her system. We now consider the subject of Baptism.

1. Divine Authority. This is found in Christ's explicit command in the great commission recorded in Matthew 28.19-20 and Mark 16.15-16. Making disciples (a better rendering would be "instructing in discipleship" as representing the verb *matheteuo),* baptising and teaching form a composite charge no part of which is to be disregarded or considered of minor importance.

2. Apostolic Practice. In the book of Acts the order stated in our Lord's mandate is invariably followed (2.41; 8.12, 36-38; 18.8). For "making disciples" see 14.21, RV. In the New Testament unbaptized believers are never contemplated.

3. Proper Subjects. All professing believers were baptized and *no others.* In present-day circumstances with so much easy profession it is advisable to have confirmatory evidence of true conversion before baptizing. In many mission fields this has been found absolutely necessary. Too hurried an acceptance of an applicant may prove an actual hindrance to his spiritual progress.

4. Appointed Method. This is plainly shown by the meaning of the word and by the significance of the rite. "Baptize" is really a transliteration of the Greek verb, which comes from *bapto*, to dip (Lk 16.24; Jn 13.26) and *baptizo*, an intensified form. These words never mean to sprinkle or to pour. All standard lexicons agree as to this and scripture use abundantly confirms it (Acts 8.38; Jn 3.23). Seeing the rite symbolizes death, burial and resurrection with Christ it necessarily involves immersion and emersion. Sprinkling a few grains of soil upon a corpse or even the pouring out of a quantity of earth upon it cannot by any argument constitute a burial! Even so the mere sprinkling or pouring of water upon a person cannot rightly be called baptism.

The question of correct formula is occasionally raised. Matthew 28.19-20 makes clear that the directions given are in force until "the end of the age" (JND). Scriptures such as Acts 2.38 and 10.48 do not contradict this. They indicate that the converts were baptized on the authority of the Lord Jesus ("in His name") or, when the preposition *eis* is used, that they were brought thus into open association with Christ (8.16; 19.5), involving adherence to the doctrine of Matthew 28.19. The Word of God, therefore, does not recognise different modes of baptism.

5. Doctrinal Import. The basic teaching is that of identification with Christ. The believer's standing before God is "in Christ" a new creation (2 Cor 5.17). God looks upon him as having shared Christ's death, burial and resurrection, so fittingly symbolized in water baptism. The "old man", that is, the Adam nature, with all its deeds has been judged, sentenced and executed in the cross of Christ, buried out of God's sight, and the believer himself is viewed as a "new man" introduced into the sphere of resurrection life with Christ (Eph 2.5-6). Accordingly, he is responsible henceforth to walk in "newness of life", reckoning himself to have died unto sin and to be alive unto God, yielding his bodily members as instruments of righteousness (Rom 6.3-13). In submitting to the rite of baptism the believer publicly confesses his acceptance of God's viewpoint and faith's resolve to live in accordance therewith.

6. Prevalent Malpractices.

(a) *Infant Sprinkling.* As we have seen, this is not true baptism. Actually it arises from ancient pagan practices. Moreover it is associated with the destructive heresy of baptismal regeneration, which teaches that an infant or adult thereby becomes "a child of God, a member of Christ and an inheritor of the Kingdom of Heaven". Multitudes have been led to trust in a ceremony instead of exercising personal faith in the Lord Jesus Christ for salvation.

(b) *Household Baptism.* This error seeks to convey the idea that persons so baptised are brought into a place of special privilege and blessing. Exponents compare it to the Jewish rite of circumcision under the Old Covenant but this is a false analogy. It was natural birth that determined a Jew's nationality and this was followed according to divine decree by a distinctive sign of relationship. In like manner, it is the new birth which determines a believer's heavenly citizenship and baptism is the divinely-appointed public sign. In neither case does the rite itself procure the coveted privilege. Circumcision does not make a Jew, for it is practised by certain other Eastern peoples. Likewise, baptism does not make a Christian (Acts 8.13; 1 Cor 10.1-6; Rom 2.28-29). Examples of baptized households are mentioned - Acts 10.44-48; 16.14-15; 29-34; 18.8; 1 Corinthians 1.16 with 16.15. That infants were included is a wholly unwarrantable assumption for note particularly Acts 16.32-34 and 18.8. If persons are old enough to "hear the word", "believe" and "rejoice" in salvation then they are old enough to be baptized.

(c) *Baptism Repudiated.* Certain sects teach that water baptism is now wholly unnecessary and that the baptism of the Holy Spirit alone is essential. These Christian friends surely forget that our Lord specifically enjoined the rite. Acts 10.45-47 records the conversion of Cornelius and a group of relatives and friends - all Gentiles. Having clear evidence that they had received the Holy Spirit, Peter directs that all should be baptized in water. Without doubt the work was assigned to the six Jewish-Christian brethren who had accompanied the apostle from Joppa (now known as Jaffa).

(d) *Rebaptizing Superfluous.* Some hold that if a person has been sprinkled or immersed before conversion rebaptizing is needless. Acts 19.4-5 does not support this view. Paul's pertinent questions reveal that these disciples had imperfect knowledge and experience of the truth. John the Baptist's teaching obviously could not have included the full facts of Christ's death, resurrection and ascension followed by the bestowal of the Holy Spirit. On hearing the full gospel from the lips of Paul, they were baptized in (or, unto) the name of the Lord Jesus.

7. **Misunderstood Texts.**

(a) *John 3.5.* In the New Testament baptism is never directly connected with the new birth. Our Lord is here referring to Ezekiel 36.24-27 and 37.1-14. The prophet shows that the application of "water" and the operation of the Holy Spirit were both necessary to the rebirth of Israel as a nation under the terms of the New Covenant. Nicodemus, "the teacher of Israel" (Jn 3.10, RV), should have understood these things. The Lord explains to him that entrance into the kingdom of God is upon the same basis. The sprinkling of water points back to Numbers 8.7; 19.1-22; cp. Hebrews 9.13-14. It typifies the application to the soul of the word of God in the gospel (1 Pet 1.23, 25; cp. Tit 3.5; Eph 5.26).

(b) *Acts 2.38.* Far from repudiating the ordinance of water baptism there are certain groups of professing Christians who go to the other extreme and maintain that it is essential to salvation. The doctrine is based principally upon Mark 16.16; Acts 2.38 and 22.16, and the very many Scriptures which teach salvation by faith in the Son of God alone, are conveniently ignored. Mark 16.16 indicates the normal accompaniment and public sign of believing, hence the words "and is not baptized" do not occur after "believeth not". It is a grave mistake to apply to Gentiles the formula given in Acts 2.38, for it belonged specifically to the Jews of that day, during a period that was transitional in the history of the Church of Christ. This may be readily inferred from the manner of the apostle's address on the day of Pentecost. Note the words, "Ye men of Israel", and "Let all the house of Israel know" (vv.22, 36). Compare the style of address at 3.12; 4.10; 5.30-31; 7.2,51. These Jews are directly charged with the crucifixion of Messiah. Observe the frequent repetition of the pronoun "ye" in 2.23; 3.13-15; 4.10; 5.30 and 7.52. The manner of approach to Gentiles with the order seen in Acts 10.34-38 is followed throughout the later Acts period and has continued down to the present day. Gentiles are not directly charged with Christ's crucifixion, for the pronoun "they" (the Jew) is used. With further reference to Acts 2.38 and 22.16 note that the emphasis is placed upon repentance, not only of their sins in general but of the particularly heinous sin of rejecting and crucifying Messiah. By being baptized such as did repent would thus publicly dissociate themselves from the great national sin and signify their adherence to Jesus as Messiah. Saul of Tarsus in a similar way was called upon to make a public renunciation of his past life of hostility to Christ and His followers. Water can never wash away sins (Heb 9.22). When used in its metaphorical sense "washing" can only bear the meaning given. This is confirmed by 1 Corinthians 6.11 RVm.

(c) *1 Corinthians 1.13-17.* When evangelizing in the city of Corinth, Paul refrained from several legitimate things on the ground that they were not expedient, that is, not profitable to his hearers, as events proved. It is apparent that the apostle usually left the actual baptizing of converts to others lest a party spirit and pride should be engendered. It would be well for home evangelists and foreign missionaries when possible to follow his example. The converts were not Paul's but Christ's; cp. John 4.2.

(d) *1 Corinthians 15.29.* This verse gives one of the concluding arguments for the truth of resurrection. The supposed early practice of persons being baptized on behalf of Christian relatives or friends who died before the rite had been performed, finds no support in authentic history, and can be dismissed as an interpretation of the passage. Among reputable Christian scholars either one or the other of the following explanations has found favour. Some believe the reference is to newly baptized converts. They were like courageous young recruits eagerly pressing forward to take the places of warriors who had fallen on the battle-front, particularly martyred believers. They were baptized "in the place of" or "in succession to" (*huper*) the latter. If there be no resurrection such courage would be displayed in vain for nothing would be gained by it either now or hereafter. Others understand the argument to be that if there be no resurrection then baptism is reduced to a meaningless ceremony, a ceremony in the interests of (*huper*) a lot of dead people, now dead spiritually and soon to be dead physically with no hope beyond the grave. Either of these explanations seems to suit the context.

(e) *1 Peter 3.20-21.* Noah's ark in the Old Testament and baptism in the New Testament are corresponding figures of God's way of salvation by faith alone. The believer commits himself to the Saviour as Noah and his family did to the ark and were borne safely through the judgement. Noah's family was separated from the older creation and stepped out upon fresh covenant terms in a "new" world. So is it in the spiritual experience of the Christian.

8. Other Baptisms. These must be carefully distinguished from Christian baptism.

(a) *Ceremonial Purifications.* Another but allied Greek word (*baptismos*) is generally used for these (Mk 7.4, 8; Heb 6.2; 9.10). However the verb *baptizo is* found at Mark 7.4, and Luke 11.38.

(b) *John's Baptism* was unto confession and repentance (Mt 3.6,11) preparatory to the advent of Messiah through whose blood-shedding alone could come "remission of sins". John's commission was a unique one (Mal 3.1; Jn 1.33).

(c) *Christ's Baptism* (Mt 3.3-17). Because of its attendant circumstances this marked Him out as the true Messiah (Jn 1.31-34). In submitting to this rite He identified Himself with the people of God. The cross finally established His claims (1 Jn 5.6; cp. Amplified New Testament).

(d) *Disciple's Baptism* (Jn 3.22, 26 with 4.1-2). This baptism signified a confession of, and adherence to, Jesus as Messiah, but not all so baptized continued to follow Him (Jn 6.66; 7.31ff).

(e) *Baptism of Suffering* (Mk 10.38-39; Lk 12.50). Our Lord refers here to His immersion in the deep soul-experience of the cross when He was overwhelmed by the billows of divine judgment vicariously endured in behalf of His believing people. The later deaths of James and John were not vicarious, of course, but these apostles were granted the privilege of suffering in fellowship with their Lord.

(f) *Baptism of the Holy Spirit* (Jn 1.33; Mk 1.8; 1 Cor 12.13). Our Lord's promise recorded in Acts 1.8 was fulfilled at Pentecost (Acts 2). The believers were then incorporated into a spiritual entity, a "Body" able to make increase of itself until it reached full maturity (Eph 4.13,16). Each individual believer upon his exercise of faith in the Saviour, our Lord Jesus Christ, is sealed for God by the Holy Spirit (Eph 1.13). At the same time he is baptized into the one "Body" by the Spirit (1 Cor 12.13) and indwelt by the Spirit (Rom 8.9,11), who is received as an earnest (a pledge - *arrabon*) of the inheritance to come (Eph 1.14; 2 Cor 1.22; 5.5). After the initial act at conversion no such thing as a later or "second" baptism of the Spirit can be experienced by the Christian, but a repeated filling may be his (Acts 2.4 with 4.31; 13.52; Eph 5.18).

(g) *Baptism of Fire* (Mt 3.11; Lk 3.16). This points neither to Pentecost nor to a Christian's individual experience but to future judgment as the verses which follow so clearly show; cp. Matthew 13.42, 50; 2 Thessalonians 1.8.

It will be observed that (e) to (g) exhibit metaphorical uses of the word "baptism".

9. **Brief Summary.** We see then that baptism is:

(a) *An Act of Submission.* It is obedience to the Lord's clear command.

(b) *An Act of Confession.* It owns the lordship of Christ in a public acknowledgment (Rom 10.9; cp. Gal 3.27). It is like a soldier who dons the Queen's uniform after enlistment. The uniform does not make him a soldier but it makes his calling evident to all.

(c) *An Act of Identification.* It symbolizes the believer's death, burial and resurrection with Christ, subsequently to walk with and serve the Lord on earth, the while his spiritual life is hid with Christ in God (Col 3.1-3) and its true sphere is in "the heavenlies".

(d) *An Act of Proclamation.* Through the medium of "eye-gate" baptism sets the basic facts of the gospel before the on-lookers (1 Cor 15.3-4).

CHAPTER THREE

THE LORD'S SUPPER

The Lord's Supper" (1 Cor 11.20) is also termed "breaking of bread" (Acts 2.42), which was primarily a common expression for partaking of a meal. It is so used in Acts 2.46; 20.11; 27.35-36; cp. Mark 6.41, etc. "Bread" is literally "loaf", for the dividing of which Jews did not use a knife. Later "the breaking of the loaf" came to have particular reference to the observance of the Lord's Supper. "Eucharist" is a non-scriptural term, but it closely connects with one of the principal acts at the Supper, namely thanksgiving (*eucharistia*). Except for its ritualistic associations it could not be considered objectionable. The same may be said of "Holy Communion", a term based upon 1 Corinthians 10.16. It expresses certain aspects of the Supper.

INSTITUTION. In the New Testament there are four records of this. Matthew 26.26-30 gives the dispensational order, Mark 14.22-26 the chronological order, Luke 22.14-23 the moral order, and 1 Corinthians 11.17-34 the memorial order. With three other passages relating thereto (Acts 2.42; 20.7; 1 Cor 10.16-17) there are seven references in all. Our Lord's command, "This do", was twice spoken and is thrice recorded.

EXEMPLIFICATION. The practice of the early disciples is clearly indicated in Scriptures already referred to. Writings from sub-apostolic times frequently refer to the importance of the ordinance and show the universality of its observance among Christians. The churches soon departed from the simplicity of the original pattern, however, and there gradually developed in certain circles a highly elaborate ritual often associated with definitely idolatrous practices. It should be noted that the breaking of bread is a collective exercise to be continued regularly, whereas baptism is a single initiatory rite for the individual believer.

PARTICIPATION. Only true believers in our Lord Jesus Christ are entitled to partake of the Lord's Supper. Participation by doubtful adherents and known unbelievers as thereby receiving the very "means of grace" is wholly contrary to sound doctrine. Acts 20.7 mentions "the disciples". Acts 2.41-42 states, "They that gladly received his word were baptized ... and they continued steadfastly ... in the breaking of bread". Incidentally we may point out other terms designating the same class, namely "believers" (Acts 5.14), "Christians" (11.26), "brethren" (11.29), and "saints" (Rom 1.7). Only believers sound in the faith and consistent in walk should be welcomed (1 Cor 5.11; 2 Jn vv.9-11; Tit 3.10-11; 2 Thess 3.6, 14). If evidence of these requirements be forthcoming there is no warrant in God's Word for imposing any further restriction whatsoever. On the other hand, it is certainly not consistent with godly order to issue a general invitation to an assembled company for anyone who wishes to participate. There should be real personal exercise of heart on the part of each believer concerned.

SIGNIFICATION. This may be exhibited in a seven-fold way. The Lord's Supper is:

1. **A Gathering of His Church** (1 Cor 11.17-21). The breaking of bread is not a subordinate gathering or a mere appendage to some other service. On the contrary it is the normal gathering of believers, the very central feature of the Christian order of worship. Acts 20.7 is strongly supported by 1 Corinthians 11-14 in which the word translated "come together" occurs just seven times and nowhere else in the New Testament of a meeting of the church. In Troas the disciples ("we", RV) gathered for the express purpose of breaking bread. They did not gather to listen to the well-known missionary Paul. Remembrance of the Lord was the governing thought in the hearts and minds of the believers. In denominational churches the focus of "divine service" or "public worship" is upon the sermon, which is not worship in the scriptural sense at all. The Supper fittingly expresses the oneness of the Body of Christ, the Church, in the spiritual union of its individual members with the risen Head in heaven and with one another. It also demonstrates

the communion flowing therefrom (1 Cor 10.16-17, RVm). Note the double significance of the one loaf, first as symbolizing our Lord's own precious body (1 Cor 11.24), then as setting forth in figure His mystic Body, the Church (1 Cor 10.16-17). In this latter passage the reversed order of cup and loaf gives the order of the believer's experience, namely appropriation of the merits of Christ's atoning blood (the cup) followed by the resulting membership in the Body of Christ (Eph 1.22-23). 1 Corinthians 11 presents the order of observance.

2. **A Memorial of His Person** (1 Cor 11.24-25, RV). The Lord's injunction ("This do") shows that the occasion is not simply one of retrospection but is an act of celebration and, be it noted, not of His death only but of Him ("for a remembrance of me"). We should not compare the observance to a memorial service for a long-dead national hero or a notable martyr in some great cause. Saints gather on the first day of the week, the Lord's resurrection day, not on the day of His death. Moreover, ours is a joyful celebration of One who, having accomplished the atoning work of the cross, rose triumphant from the tomb and ascended to the right hand of God. He is commemorated, therefore, not as a long-absent One so much as One who ever lives and is present according to His gracious promise (Mt 18.20).

3. **A Token of His Love** (1 Cor 11.23). It was the night in which He was betrayed that our Lord instituted the Supper, yet His thoughts were more upon His sorrowing disciples than upon His own sufferings; see John 13.1. Love delights to serve and to give (Mt 20.28; Lk 22.19; Jn 10.11), and is measured by the extent of its sacrifice. As we partake of His Supper, the Lord is afforded an opportunity to impart a further impulse to our devotion in a fresh realization of His love.

4. **A Pledge of His Covenant** (1 Cor 11.25; Lk 22.20). Every divine covenant mentioned in Scripture has its distinctive sign. For instance, the sign of the Mosaic Covenant given to Israel was the weekly sabbath (Ex 31.13, 17; Ezek 20.12, 20). The sign of the New Covenant is the cup of which we partake at the Supper, for it symbolizes our Saviour's blood shed in ratification of it (Heb 9.15-22). For further teaching on the New Covenant see Hebrews 7.22; 8.6-13; 10.16-18; 12.24; 13.20 and 2 Corinthians 3.6-18.

5. **A Partaking of His Feast** (1 Cor 11.26 - "eat ... drink"). Some are averse from referring to the Supper as a feast. Rightly understood, however, there seems to be no valid objection. It is surely a fitting occasion for us to express the joy of reconciliation to God (Lk 15.22-24), reconciliation made possible only on the ground of the death for us of His Son (Rom 5.10-11). We may compare the significance of the peace-offering (Lev 3 and 7), the offerer with his family and friends feasting upon the divinely-allotted portion of the sacrifice in joyful realization of reconciliation to God. Four imperatives indicate a personal partaking of both loaf and cup, "Take - eat - drink - do". The Supper is symbolic also of a broader concept, the Lord's Table (1 Cor 10.21). These are not interchangeable terms though we often treat them as such. The "table" represents fellowship in all the gracious provision the Lord has made for His redeemed people. At this "table" the believer is always "sitting" (cp. Ps 23.5), but only at appointed times does he sit at the Lord's Supper. 1 Corinthians 10 contrasts the "table of the Lord" with the "table of demons", which latter stands for all the worldly provision the devil makes for His devotees, even in the moral and religious spheres. The Christian is to have no fellowship whatever with such. He should do nothing to compromise his testimony for God before the world or to stumble a weaker brother (see context). At the Supper Christ Himself is the unseen Host and Ruler of the feast (cp. Jn 2.9). The "table" which speaks of abundant grace and generous sufficiency (2 Sam 9.7, 10-11, 13), though so free to us was spread by our Lord at infinite cost to Himself.

6. **A Proclamation of His Death** (1 Cor 11.26, RV). The AV word "shew" has been misunderstood and is often cited as "shew forth". The Greek (*kataggello*), however, indicates not representation but proclamation, not showing to God but witnessing to men, the gospel in object lesson (1 Cor 15.3-4). The same Greek word is used at 2.1; 9.14 and elsewhere in the NT in the sense "to preach". We have already seen that baptism also is a gospel testimony through eye-gate, the emphasis being upon Christ's resurrection, whilst the Supper stresses His death. The combined witness of the two ordinances is very weighty. It

has been pointed out that the announcing is in the eating and drinking (text). We may perhaps see the death of Christ already set forth in the separation of loaf and cup, representing His body and His blood respectively. The fact of His death and the significance of it are both announced in carrying out the ordinance.

7. **A Prophecy of His Coming** (1 Cor 11.26). "Till He come" is Paul's inspired comment. Here is the glorious consummation for which the saints look. It sets a limit to the period of observance and is also clear indication that obedience to this command of the Lord must not be neglected in the waiting time. As the well-known hymn has it

"Backward look we drawn to Calvary musing while we sing;
Forward haste we to Thy coming, Lord and King!

CELEBRATION. The keynote here is *simplicity* according to the scriptural pattern. Departure is seen almost everywhere in Christendom, grievous errors and ritualistic practices having obscured the original meaning and purpose. Loose observance also destroys the true character of the Supper (1 Cor 11.20ff). At first it was observed by Christians in connexion with a social meal, later called a love-feast (*agape*) (Jude v.12; 2 Pet 2.13, RV; 1 Cor 11.21-22). Acts 2.46 probably indicates a necessary arrangement owing to numbers. For worship the Christians still gathered with the rest of the Jews in the temple. The practice shows also that the early communal order did not involve the break-up of family life. The appearance of abuses as well as other considerations led ultimately to the separation of the Lord's Supper from ordinary and social meals (1 Cor 11.34). The word of God avoids laying down laws of celebration. Scope is thus given to Christian devotion and liberty.

1. **Day and Time.** The words "as oft" (1 Cor 11.25) and "as often" (next verse) imply frequent observance, not once or thrice yearly or even monthly. Acts 20.7 indicates a regular practice of meeting on the first day of the week for the specific purpose of breaking bread. Paul had arrived at Troas the previous Monday and although his journey was an urgent one (v.16) he patiently waited until the ensuing Lord's Day for the breaking of bread gathering of the church, after which he departed

without further loss of time (vv.11,13). It is significant that our Lord first appeared to gathered disciples on His resurrection day and on successive first days of the week. The first day symbolizes the new creation day, whereas the Jewish Sabbath (seventh day) looked back to the old creation order. Linking the Lord's Supper and the Lord's Day is the Greek word *kuriakos* (pertaining to a lord) occurring but twice in the New Testament (1 Cor 11.20; Rev 1.10). Further support as to the special character of this first day is found in 1 Corinthians 16.1-2. The word "supper" does not determine the time of day. The Greek word so translated is a more general term, in the New Testament sometimes indicating a social meal especially in celebration of an important event. It is fitting that the remembrance "feast" should have first place in collective Christian worship.

2. **Elements.** Controversy among believers over the composition of the elements used should be avoided. In certain places bitter feelings have been aroused leading even to division. How grieving this must be to the Spirit of the Lord! It was at the Passover meal that Christ instituted His Supper, but the two must never be confounded. He took a "loaf" of bread and a cup of wine as simple elements ready to hand. Emphasis in the New Testament is never on "bread" and "wine" but always on "loaf" and "cup" as fitting symbols of Christ's vicarious death. Nowadays these elements are already set aside before we gather. In Scripture no lesson is drawn either from the composition of the loaf or the contents of the cup, though we ourselves may find some interesting and helpful suggestions. The wisdom of this arrangement is more readily appreciated in lands where wheaten loaves and grape wine are not always obtainable. The modern practice in some quarters of using cut wafers and individual cups quite destroys the true significance of the Supper as a communion of the one Body of Christ.

3. **Distribution.** In the passage regulating the order of Christian gathering (1 Cor 11 to 14) it is important to notice that no president, whether leading elder or other "official", is seen. The claim to have special authority to dispense the elements entirely alters the character of the Supper and is plainly contrary to the Word of God.

Even the apostles had no official status in this respect. They simply took their place with the rest of the saints. Acts 20.11 provides no exception for it refers to the taking of an ordinary meal. The verbs are all in the singular number and denote individual acts by the apostle. Luke and others had already departed, it seems, to go aboard ship (v.13). Clerisy today is strongly entrenched behind the unscriptural practice of permitting only so-called ordained ministers or other appointed persons to "officiate".

4. Regulation. In the chapters already referred to Paul deals with disorders in the gatherings of the church at Corinth and gives divine regulations for the observance of the Lord's Supper and the use of spiritual gifts. That one gathering is primarily contemplated after the pattern of Acts 20.7 is here shown by the use of characteristic words such as "come together" (*sunerchomai*, occurring seven times and nowhere else in the New Testament concerning the church); "give thanks" (*eucharisteo*, 1 Cor 14.16-17 with 11.24); "whole assembly" (1 Cor 14.23). The Holy Spirit is not mentioned in 1 Corinthians after 12.13. He retires from view, so to speak, in favour of the Lord Jesus, who is recognized in the midst as Head of His Church and Host at His Supper; cp. John 16.14. On the other hand, the personal responsibility of those taking part is emphasized by the use of imperative forms of verbs no less than twenty-one times in ch. 14. The often heard expression "the leading of the Spirit" appears only twice in the New Testament (Rom 8.14 and Gal 5.18), and is connected with the believer's walk, not with worship. However, if not walking by the Spirit during the week one cannot expect to be led of the Spirit at the Supper. The Holy Spirit's prompting is not by some supernatural impulse, not by unintelligent zeal, and certainly not by fleshly desire to display gift. These errors were all seen in the church at Corinth. Moreover, taking audible part must not be mere emotional exercise but is to be by spiritual understanding and spiritual discernment of spiritual persons (1 Cor 14.14-15, 19-20).

Although the regulation of order is seen primarily in connexion with "tongues" and "prophecy", gifts which have now ceased (13.8), seven underlying principles are discernible; (a) not everyone is to take part (v.26 is ironical); (b) messages are to be limited to two or three and to be given in turn (vv.27, 31); (c) speech must be in language both heard and understood (vv.6-11); (d) consideration should be given to other gifted persons present (vv.30-31); (e) gift is to be under self-control (vv.32-33), the appropriateness or otherwise of what is spoken being judged by others, not by the speaker himself (v.29); (f) the constant aim of speakers must be the edification of the saints, a "building up" not a "pulling down" ministry (vv.12,26), always remembering that five words in season may encourage the spirit of worship (v.19), whereas much vain talking is quite out of place (1 Tim 1.3-7; Tit 1.9); finally, (g) everything is to be conducted in a seemly manner and be fully appropriate to the occasion (v.40). See 2 Corinthians 3.17 and note that liberty means neither licence nor legality, which are both manifestations of fleshly activity. Persistent offenders against the divine order ought to be firmly dealt with by the assembly elders. If the fault be merely one of unintelligent zeal, the erring one should be corrected in a spirit of patient grace.

5. **Procedure.** Breaking the loaf has no ceremonial meaning. It is simply for the convenience of those assembled, especially if the loaf is large and crusty, otherwise it need not be broken before being passed round. All "break" the bread in the sense of partaking (1 Cor 10.16-17). Our Lord's body was not broken (Jn 19.36; 1 Cor 11.24, RV). Similarly, with pouring the wine where such is done. No special significance attaches to this act. All ritual order and use of some particular formula should be avoided. Insistence upon details of no importance only genders strife (2 Tim 2.23; Tit 3.9). As with the gospel meeting and all other gatherings of the church, there is nothing secret about the observance of the Lord's Supper, in marked contrast with the practices of Masonic and other Lodges, which originate in the ancient mystery cults of paganism. It is of interest to note the incidental reference to "many lights" in Acts 20.8; cp. 1 Corinthians 14.23-25.

6. **Preparation.** 1 Corinthians 11.27-32 is a passage of solemn import. Corinthian excesses may not occur today, but irreverent behaviour and meaningless formality are far too common. Distinguish between unworthy *persons* partaking and an

unworthy *manner* of partaking which latter is in view here. A divided fellowship, a discordant spirit, distracting thoughts and disturbing movements are all unworthy of the presence of the Lord. A defiled conscience also hinders remembrance and worship, therefore prior self-examination is called for and known sin judged, confessed and cleansed (1 Jn 1.9), otherwise the chastening of the Lord may be incurred. The judgment indicated in v.29 is temporal not eternal. The previous verse removes all excuse for absence. Knowledge of another's failure does not alter the obligation, "This do". If one be personally involved the procedure given in James 5.16 and Matthew 18.15ff, also the principle of Matthew 5.23-24 should be followed. Our Lord prepared His disciples for the Supper in the upper room by feet-washing, an act of deep symbolic meaning as the context shows (Jn 13.1-10).

SUPERSTITION. We have already alluded to the sad fact that many erroneous doctrines and practices have destroyed the original simplicity of the Lord's Supper. Two call for mention here.

1. **Transubstantiation.** This doctrine of the Church of Rome, introduced in AD 831, declares that "at the instant of consecration (by the officiating priest) the elements are changed into that body which was born of the virgin; the outward appearance only remains as before". The commemorative aspect is thus changed into a celebration of the idolatrous Mass, during which, at the elevation of the Host, the communicants adore Christ as being actually *present therein*. To quote further, "there is offered to God a sure, proper and propitiatory sacrifice for the living and the dead". This is sheer blasphemy! A most ornate ritual so attractive to the flesh accompanies the performance. Contrast Hebrews 7.27; 9.14; 10.10-14.

2. **Consubstantiation** is a Lutheran doctrine dating from the Reformation in the 16th century. This movement though it accomplished much, did not break free altogether from the established clerical order. Certain errors of doctrine and practice still remain in the "Reformation Churches". Consubstantiation teaches that Christ is bodily *present with* the elements at the moment of partaking.

MISCONCEPTION. Certain Scriptures are often misapplied to the Lord's Supper. John 6.48-58 has no direct reference thereto, for the Supper had not then been instituted. It has to do with the appropriation of Christ by faith for eternal life (v.54). 1 Corinthians 5.7-8 does not point to the Lord's Supper - see RVm. Passover typifies the once-for-all sacrifice of Christ as the Lamb of God. The seven-day festival of Unleavened Bread which immediately followed typifies the whole round of the Christian life - a life to be kept free from all spiritual "leaven", malice in motives, and wickedness in conduct. One name, either Passover or Unleavened Bread, often covered both feasts (Lk 22.1; Mk 14.12 with Lev 23.5-6). As to the propriety of Christians breaking bread where there is no established assembly, whilst it is true that 1 Corinthians 11 gives the assembly order, this does not rule out the observance by believers in circumstances of a temporary nature, such as travelling aboard ship, etc. The promise of Matthew 18.20 may surely be appropriated by them. Christ instituted the ordinance for "disciples" before the Church was inaugurated. Moreover, breaking bread is predicated of "disciples" not of the local assembly as such (Acts 2.42; 20.7; cp. Lk 24.30,35).

SUMMARY. The believer's relation to the Lord's Supper may be described as

1. **An Act of Submission.** *Will* exercised in response to the Lord's *authority*, resulting in the joy of *obedience*.

2. **An Act of Devotion.** *Heart* exercised in response to His *love*, resulting in the joy of *mutual attachment*.

3. **An Act of Appropriation.** *Faith* exercised in response to His *grace*, resulting in the joy of *satisfaction*.

4. **An Act of Adoration.** *Spirit* exercised in response to His *deity*, resulting in the joy of *worship*.

5. **An Act of Communion.** *Brotherly love* exercised in response to His *kinship*, resulting in the joy of *fellowship*.

6. **An Act of Expectation.** *Hope* exercised in response to His *promise*, resulting in the joy of *anticipation*.

7. **An Act of Self-examination.** *Conscience* exercised in response to His *holiness*, resulting in the joy of *restoration*.

CHAPTER FOUR

WORSHIP AND PRIESTHOOD

DEFINITION. The English word "worship" comes from the earlier form "worthship". Primarily it describes an act of respect shown towards a person of merit. To worship is to pay homage to, or hold in high honour, someone who is worthy. In the highest sense it means to approach God with supreme respect and veneration. Divine worship is nowhere in Scripture actually defined, but its import may be gathered from certain words employed and from examples recorded. Words used are:

(a) *proskuneo,* to prostrate oneself (lit. kiss) towards, to pay homage (Mt 8.2, etc.). It denotes the outward act with or without a corresponding inward attitude.

(b) *sebomai,* to revere, to feel awe for (e.g. Acts 16.14) expresses an inward attitude. Kindred words are found in Romans 1.25; Acts 17.23.

(c) *latreuo,* often translated to serve, is a wider term covering official service rendered to a superior, or religious service offered to God or to false gods (Phil 3.3; Heb 10.2; 13.10).

Examples of worship may be found Matthew 2.1-12 (the Magi); John 12.1-3 (Mary); see also 1 Chronicles 29.10-22; Deuteronomy 26.1-11. The Psalms abound in expressions of worship, providing a vocabulary that may be profitably used by Christians; see, for example, Psalms 95, 96 and 107.

DIFFERENTIATION. We should carefully distinguish between *worship,* which is God's people coming in to God with acceptable offerings, and *ministry,* which shows God coming out to His people, so to speak, with blessings to meet their needs. Worship is Godward, ministry is saintward, testimony is worldward. Distinguish also terms often used for the general idea of worship. *Prayer,* in its restricted sense, is approaching God with respect to one's need or that of others. *Thanksgiving* is acknowledging blessings received from God. *Praise* is appreciating God on account of His works, acts being in view (Ps 103). *Worship* in the strict sense is adoring God on account of His essential worthiness, attributes being in view (Ps 104).

EXPRESSION. Worship is the highest duty and privilege of God's redeemed people. It is properly a continual exercise, the normal attitude of soul towards God rather than a series of isolated acts (Heb 13.15; cp. Ps 34.1-3). If one is not a worshipper during the week and when alone, it is hardly likely one will be so in the company of believers on the Lord's Day. Here is fruit of the new life in Christ, an expression of happy relationship to God established in redeeming and restoring grace, for worship can flow only from the hearts of those who have a sure knowledge of salvation through faith in the Son of God. Unregenerate persons cannot worship God. Man must be a receiver of God's gift, the living water of the Spirit, before he can worship in spirit and truth (Jn 4.10-14, 23-24). Only believers now are constituted a holy and royal priesthood to offer up spiritual sacrifices (1 Pet 2.4-10). Saints of old worshipped God as Jehovah, the covenant God. Christians worship God as Father. The former were taught to seek Jehovah. In the present day of grace it is the Father who seeks worshippers (Jn 4.23). Worship of the Father takes place in the holy intimacy of the divine family circle. His children approach Him with reverent love, from the youngest to the oldest all having access to Him on equal footing. Such privilege saints of Old Testament times never knew, although individually many rose to a high level of spiritual experience in communion with God. In the circle of the divine family, Christ, firstborn among many brethren, Himself is the Precentor leading the praises (Heb 2.10-13). From this holy exercise even "babes" in Christ are not excluded (Mt 21.16 with 11.25-26).

Worship needs to conform to the nature of God (Jn 4.20-24). He is Spirit, therefore worship must be spiritual; cp. Acts 17.24-25. Israel had the "shadow" in the types, and acts of worship were chiefly in the realm of the material. The Christian has the "substance", the reality in the person of Christ, and worship is in the realm of the spiritual (Hebrews 8.5; 10.1; Col 2.16-17). All formality therefore is excluded. As a spiritual act worship requires the prompting of our spirits by the Holy Spirit, who is the sole power for worship (Phil 3.3). The flesh is wholly incapable of it. The human spirit is the highest part of man's tripartite being and by it the believer is able to apprehend divine things (1 Thess 5.23; 1 Cor 2.11-12).

Collective worship is indicated in Hebrews 10.19-25; 1 Corinthians 14.15-17, etc., and is seen to be associated with the gathering of the assembly for the breaking of bread (1 Cor 11). The spirit and the understanding are then both in exercise, the whole assembly uniting in the joyful liberty of the Holy Spirit to offer praise and thanksgiving to God through the Lord Jesus Christ. All human arrangement hinders the free operation of God's Spirit. In the exercise of his priestly privilege any brother present potentially may take audible part remembering, of course, that he voices the worship of the whole assembly and not simply his own individual feelings. Worship being a most solemn exercise, an attitude of reverence before, during and after the assembling should be maintained.

Worship is hindered by guilt upon the conscience, hence the need of self-examination before the meeting. All the while David's sin remained unconfessed, his praise was silent. He could utter only cries of distress and of complaint (Ps 51.3-5 with 32.3-5).

In no Christian function have fleshly expedients intruded more than in the worship of God. Divine order has been displaced in so-called "public worship" or "divine service" by human formularies. Such religious services commonly use a liturgy, which is often heedlessly hurried through by a mixed company of believers and unbelievers, with the sermon as the central feature. This is not true worship. Outward forms serve only to cover inward failure. Use of means that appeal to the aesthetic sense of the congregation, such as ornate buildings, imposing ceremonies, affecting music, and eloquent sermonizing on topics of the day, all betray a sad, carnal condition. It is like the "strange fire" offered by Nadab and Abihu, sons of Aaron (Lev 10.1-2). Sooner or later it will call down the judgment of God, for such spurious worship dishonours His holy name. Multitudes of nominal Christians are like the Samaritans, of whom the Lord declared, "Ye worship that which ye know not" (RV), or, as Weymouth's translation renders it, "You worship One of whom you know nothing" (Jn 4.22).

PARTICIPATION. The subject of worship can be better understood by tracing the history of priesthood in the Scriptures, for worship is inseparably connected therewith. The first priest spoken of as such is Melchizedek, but the office was already in existence. Prior to the Christian priesthood we may distinguish in the Old Testament four orders:

1. *Patriarchal Priesthood,* the family order. Examples are Noah (Gen 8.20-21); Abraham (Gen 12.7-8); Isaac (Gen 26.25; 31.54); Jacob (Gen 35.1-3, 7); Job (1.5 and 42.8).

2. *Royal Priesthood,* the Melchizedek order (Gen 14.18-20). This king was a unique type of Christ enthroned in heaven (Heb 7), and as King-Priest upon the throne of David in the coming millennial age (Zech 6.12-13).

3. *National Priesthood,* the world order (Ex 19.5-6). It was offered conditionally to Israel as a chosen nation, but owing to sad failure they forfeited this special favour (Hos 4.6). However, God's purpose is not thereby frustrated, but only postponed till a future day (Is 61.6; Ezek 44.15-16). Meanwhile Christian priesthood fills the privileged position (1 Pet 2.5-9).

4. *Levitical Priesthood,* the Aaronic order (Lev 8). This was strictly limited to Aaron and his family. Even the near-of-kin Levites were excluded (Num 16.8-10; cp. 2 Chr 26.16-21). In appointment Christ's high priesthood is after the Melchizedek

order but His service follows in many respects the Aaronic pattern. The Hebrew Epistle brings out both similarities and contrasts. Christians as associated with Christ in the priesthood find a rich storehouse of instruction in the detailed types seen in the record of the Aaronic family.

5. *Spiritual Priesthood,* the Christian order (1 Pet 2.5-9; Rev 1.6). We are priests whose glorious destiny is disclosed in Revelation 5.8-10 and 4.10-11. In the latter passage worship is based upon creation, in the former upon redemption. Revelation 1.6 refers to the contextual millennial age. The Christian priesthood consists of all true believers during this present day of grace (1 Pet 2.7). Such are "born anew" (1.23; 2.2) and are "living stones" in a spiritual house (2.5). Unlike the Levitical order there is now no distinction between the sexes or between youth and age, except that the *audible* expression of worship (apart from singing) in the assembly is restricted to brethren (1 Cor 14.34; see 1 Chr 23.13 with Lev 8; Ex 28.1). The New Testament knows nothing of a sacerdotal class or clergy distinct from the so-called "laity". Recognition of such a group wearing characteristic dress and claiming special rank and privilege violates the Christian order altogether.

The basis of worship is an experience of redemption. Israel could not worship in Egypt (Ex 3.18; 5.1-3). It was after God had brought them out that the system of divine worship was established. We note that in the typical order qualified priests were *called* (Ex 28.1; Heb 5.1, 4; 1 Pet 2.9); *cleansed* (Lev 8.6); *clothed* (Lev 8.13; Ex 28.40 - the distinctive garments bearing evidence of their special calling even as a Christian's conduct should do); and *consecrated,* set apart for holy service first by the application of blood (Lev 8.24), then by the sprinkling of oil with blood (v.30). Every detail has its spiritual counterpart in the Christian priesthood. In Hebrew to consecrate means literally "to fill the hands". As sinners we approach God with empty hands but as worshippers it is otherwise (Deut 16.16; 26.1-10; Heb 13.15).

LOCATION (Jn 4.20-21). The Christian "place of worship" is the heavenly sanctuary not the local building in which we gather (Heb 10.19-25 with 8.1-2; 9.11-12). It is termed "within the veil" where Christ our High Priest in person now is (Heb 4.14; 9.24). God's presence-chamber is entered in spirit not in body, and by faith not by outward form. We see in Hebrews 10.19-22 a *perfect title* - the blood of Jesus; a *prepared way* - the rent veil, speaking of His violent death; and a *powerful Helper* - the Great Priest, who leads and sustains His worshipping people.

DEVOTION. The Levitical priests ministered in bare feet. The tradition is well supported by the command to Moses (Ex 3.5) and Joshua (5.15); cp. Ecclesiastes 5.1. It was the common custom when entering a house for the visitor to remove his sandals and wash his feet after even a short journey. In better class homes a slave performed both these acts in deference to the guest; cp. Luke 7.44; John 13.3-5. The priests washed both hands and feet by divine command, for they served on holy ground (Ex 30.17-21). Besides ablutions, abstinence from strong drink, abstention from mourning, and defilement by contact with the dead were also strictly enjoined. Thus we are taught that due reverence and practical holiness are essential in all who would draw near to God (Lev 10.9; 21.1; Heb 12.28-29). Physical soundness and ceremonial fulfilment were both required (Lev 21.16-24), and in like manner moral defects in a believer's life are a barrier to acceptable worship.

FUNCTION. Two main aspects of privilege connected with the activities of the Christian priesthood are brought before us in the New Testament (1 Pet 2.5,9).

1. **Holy Priests** to present offerings to God.

(a) *Privilege of Access.* Right of entry is granted to all and is unrestrained as to times, for prayer (Heb 4.16), and for worship (Heb 10.22; cp. Eph 2.13,18; 3.12). Contrast Aaronic priests to whom the outer compartment of tabernacle and temple, the holy place, alone was accessible, the holiest being barred even to the high priest except once yearly after the prescribed ritual order (Lev 16.1-2; Heb 9.6-8).

(b) *Presentation of Gifts.* Under the Levitical order these were of a material nature. Under the Christian order they are both spiritual and material; *praises* (Heb 13.15); *persons* (Rom 12.1-2); and *possessions* (Heb 13.16; Phil 4.18; 2 Cor 8.1-5). Christian giving is lifted out of the realm of a mere charitable collection.

2. **Royal Priests** to dispense God's gifts to men.

(a) *Ministry of Prayer.* We are accorded the privilege of intercession for the saints, following the example of our High Priest in heaven (Heb 7.21-24; Rom 8.34; Jas 5.16; Heb 13.18; 2 Thess 3.1), and intercession for all men, especially those occupying high station (1 Tim 2.1-2).

(b) *Ministry of Sympathy.* In this also our High Priest sets an example (Heb 4.15-16; 2.18; Rom 12.15). Spiritual help is needed more often than material aid.

(c) Ministry of Instruction (1 Pet 2.9; cp. Mal 2.7), making known the perfections of Christ, also discerning issues and deciding questions as did the Aaronic priests but in the moral sphere (Lev 10.10-11; chs. 13 and 14; Deut 17.9).

(d) *Ministry of the Gospel* (Rom 15.16). The word translated "ministering" in this verse (it occurs nowhere else in the New Testament) signifies to minister as a priest. To the Gentiles Paul's was a priestly service.

PROVISION. With respect to the gracious provision God made for His priests of old, it is most instructive to study the typical import of the prescribed portions of the sacrifices (Lev 8.31-32; Num 18.8-20, etc.) and of prohibited things (Lev 10.8-11).

CHAPTER FIVE

FELLOWSHIP

DEFINITION. The word "fellowship" denotes a mutual sharing, having a common interest in something, a partnership. The New Testament *koinonia is* also translated "communion", "communication", and cognates by allied words.

FOUNDATION. Christian fellowship is based upon a shared-by-all interest in the person and work of Christ. It is not founded upon racial affinity or social status, nor upon cultural aims or political creed, such as we find in world fellowships, brotherhoods and unions. Christian fellowship is the privilege of all who are sanctified (set apart) in Christ Jesus (1 Cor 1.2), sanctified by faith in Him (Acts 26.18) and thereby called into the fellowship of God's Son (1 Cor 1.9). Sharing a common faith (Tit 1.4) they enjoy a salvation common to all (Jude v.3). For a short period at the beginning of the Church's history they held even their possessions in the common interest (Acts 2.44-45; 4.32). This was not Communism as some allege, for it was an entirely voluntary contribution by happy mutual arrangement. Communism on the other hand compulsorily takes from one to distribute to others, an appropriation by the State of the property, powers and even persons of the people. Community of interest drew the believers together in one holy fellowship, united in worship, in witness and in well-doing (1 Jn 3.14, 16-18).

CONSTITUTION. This fellowship established by God is eternal in character, though enjoyment of it depends upon the spiritual state of the individual believer. It is active not passive, an outworking of faith in serving the Lord and His people (Jas 2.20ff; Philem vv.4,7). In some businesses there are "sleeping partners", who draw a share of the profits but do no work therein. In the Christian fellowship it should not be so. It is not simply "pew-sitting" or just sharing the Lord's Supper. Moreover true fellowship negates both "isolationism" (Heb 10.24-25; Acts 2.42), and a "butterfly" procedure of flitting about from one company of Christians to another in order, for instance, to sample teaching that is agreeable to the taste. Note the words "their own company" (Acts 4.23), and "one of you" (Col 4.9,12). This fellowship is

1. **A Fellowship with God** (1 Jn 1.1-7). Here we see

(a) *Privileged Communion* - with the Father (v. 3), who shares His beloved Son with us; with the Son who shares a knowledge of the Father with us (v. 3 with Jn 1.18); and of the Holy Spirit, who enables us to commune with God and with one another (2 Cor 13.14).

(b) *Essential Condition* is walking in the Light (vv. 5-7, cp. Eph 5.6-14; Rom 13.12). Fellowship is disrupted by sin but the way of restoration is here indicated (Jn 1.9 to 2.2).

(c) Blessed Consequence (2 Pet 1.3-4, RV). New birth is not in view here but a progressive likeness to God, hence the exhortation in the following verses; cp. 1 Peter 1.3 with vv. 15-16. A child is not only born of his parents but grows in likeness to them.

2. **A Fellowship with the Apostles** (1 Jn 1.3). Through their writings we share with them their personal knowledge of Christ, His words and His works (vv. 1-3). The doctrine of Christ (2 Jn vv.9-11) is that which embodies these facts. It is the apostolic doctrine referred to in Acts 2.42, which formed the basis of Christian fellowship.

3. **A Fellowship with the Saints.** Philippians, sometimes called the "Epistle of Joyful Fellowship" brings this out most helpfully as

(a) *A Fellowship of Salvation* (1.7). "Partakers . . . of grace" covers the whole range of spiritual blessings (Eph 1.3).

(b) *A Fellowship of Service* (1.5). For examples see 4.3; Philemon v.17; 2 Corinthians 8.23.

(c) *A Fellowship of Spirit* (2.1). In the light of the context it would seem better here to read "spirit" (small "s") denoting the Christian's spirit. This is not to deny that the Holy Spirit is the enabling power. Harmony of spirit does not mean uniformity of disposition or of action. The apostles greatly differed in character as do Christians generally.

(d) *A Fellowship of Suffering* (3.10; 1.29-30). Compare Hebrews 10.33 and Revelation 1.9; 2 Corinthians 1.5-7; 1 Peter 5.9.

(e) *A Fellowship of Substance* (4.14ff; cp. Heb 13.16). Such practical fellowship takes in not only the necessities of the poor among the saints (Rom 12.13; 15.26; 2 Cor 8.1-5; 1 Tim 6.18), but also servants of God who are not otherwise provided for (Phil 4.14-16; Gal 6.6; 1 Tim 5.17).

The Lord's Supper has been called "the focal point" of Christian fellowship; cp. 1 Corinthians 10.16-17. Neither it nor its sister ordinance baptism creates the fellowship, but they both express it. There is involved the responsibility of separation from all that is contrary to the mind of the Lord. It negates

(a) *Fellowship with demons,* such as connexion with idolatry, spiritism, error cults, etc. (1 Cor 10.18-22; 2 Jn vv.9-11).

(b) *Fellowship with the world* (1 Jn 5.19, RV). The world (*kosmos*) takes in the whole organized world-system, social, political and religious (2 Cor 6.14 to 7.1; Eph 5.10-11; 1 Jn 2.15; Rom 12.2; Jas 4.4).

(c) *Fellowship with sins* (1 Tim 5.22; Rom 13.14; 2 Jn v.11). Concerning the harlot church and her "daughters" see Revelation 18.4 with 14.8 and 17.1-6. In harmony with other Scriptures these passages surely teach that even now where apostate conditions prevail, loyal Christians should separate themselves.

RECEPTION. "Receiving into fellowship" is a much-abused phrase. According to Scripture the only possible meaning is the acknowledgment of a fellowship already existing between the individual and God. God's reception of necessity precedes man's and we should receive all whom God has received subject to the stipulations concerning sound doctrine and consistent practice (Rom 14.3). The local assembly is not like a man-organized "fellowship" into which a person may be introduced and elected by fellow-members. Reception of a believer is in the name of Christ as one who belongs to Him, not in the name of the church or upon any other ground (Rom 15.7).

Two classes of believers are recognized, namely "strong" and "weak" (Rom 15.1; 14.1ff). The strong are to support the weak not stumble them. The latter is a serious matter in the sight of the Lord (1 Thess 5.14; Rom 14.13-21; 1 Cor 8.9-13). One who is weak in faith is to be received but not to "doubtful disputations", that is, not for the purpose of probing into his opinions, or judging his scruples (Rom 14.1). Weak ones, be it noted, are believers who hold sincere scruples concerning matters of no vital importance, those who have not yet understood the "liberty wherewith Christ has made us free" (Gal 5.1). Such are the legalists, who place unnecessary restrictions upon themselves and others. How often these very persons consider themselves to be the really strong ones! Physical weakness may arise from tenderness in age, or infirmity of constitution, or from contracted sickness. So is it in the spiritual sphere. It has been well said, "The assembly should be a nursery for babes in Christ, a nursing home for the weak, and a training home for all". In God's redeemed family there are various stages of spiritual growth (1 Jn 2.12-14). There is room for all His children in happy fellowship, but no room for an intolerant spirit towards any. Weakness must be distinguished from sins. The latter are to be dealt with, the former borne with (Rom 15.1-3). Weakness is often manifested in those who have been brought up from childhood in connexion with an assembly and truly converted but not fully taught. This weakness may result from failure on the part of elders, who should see that a balanced ministry is afforded, or because of heedlessness of such ministry when given. A similar condition is sometimes found among Christians brought up in connexion with denominational churches. They find it difficult to throw off all at once wrong ideas and practices taught them in the past. When they are received, wise and gracious handling is needed, that they may be instructed in the way of the Lord more perfectly (Acts 18.25ff).

1. **New converts are received** (Acts 2.41; 5.14; 11.24; 2.47, lit. "such as were being saved"). On being baptized these converts were immediately introduced to the fellowship of local believers, and were included in all the privileges and responsibilities connected therewith (Acts 2.41-42).

2. **Christian new-comers are received** upon presenting

(a) *Letters of Commendation* from other churches or from well-known servants of God (2 Cor 3.1-2; Acts 18.27; Rom 16.1; Col 4.10; Philem vv.12,17). This principle was fully recognized by Paul though he himself personally did not need such a letter. To demand one in the case of a known and honoured servant of Christ, as has sometimes happened, is arbitrary and unwarranted (3 Jn vv.5 -8; Acts 21.17). In the case of an unknown believer a letter of commendation gives a measure of confidence as an endorsement of character from those with whom he has been in fellowship previously. We should not forget that even our Lord presented His credentials when He came among men who knew Him not (Jn 5.30-37).

(b) *Personal Introduction,* that is by someone in the assembly who can vouch for the genuineness of the new-comer (Acts 9.27).

(c) *Satisfactory Evidence.* It is not possible in all circumstances for a letter of commendation to be produced. In such cases there is great danger of unwittingly doing harm to a dear child of God by refusing to receive him or her merely for the sake of upholding a rule locally made. It is then expedient and proper for local elders to make a few inquiries, which no right-minded Christian will resent if conducted in a gracious spirit. The person concerned will surely understand the importance of maintaining godly order in the assembly. If the inquiries are satisfactory it would seem advisable for the person's name and connexions to be mentioned in the assembly so that he or she may become known to, and be accorded a welcome by, those in the assembly. In the case of Christians proposing to link themselves more or less permanently with the assembly, time should be given for possible objection to be made which, of course, must be upon valid, that is, scriptural grounds. Elders do well to inquire of one coming from another assembly without a letter of commendation whether he or she is under discipline. No one in this position should be received, at least until full investigation has been made. A better way then would be to persuade the person to seek first a reconciliation with that assembly. Experience shows that few persons having ulterior motives will attempt to associate themselves with a scripturally-conducted assembly. Exceptions should be dealt with as the need arises, that is, when moral or doctrinal evil manifests itself (Acts 8.21). A person's reputation for good or evil often precedes his coming, and in other cases it shows up later (1 Tim 5.24-25). Elders are responsible to guard the assembly from erroneous teaching and moral evil, but must not go beyond this to impose restrictions upon a Christian's liberty to act as he believes the Word of God allows in matters of expediency. Although elders take the lead they should ever remember that it is not they who receive or put away, but the assembly as a whole (1 Cor 5.4). The arbitrary action of Diotrephes was a virtual denial of the Lordship of Christ (3 Jn v.9).

For assembly fellowship there should be evidence of salvation, soundness of doctrine, and consistency in life. Baptism alone is no test. An unbaptized believer is as much a child of God and a member of the Body of Christ as a baptized one. A baptized unbeliever is neither. Baptism is no more essential to fellowship than it is to salvation, though necessary to obedience in common with other of our Lord's commands. Nevertheless, an over-eagerness to partake of the Lord's Supper with a manifest reluctance to do His will in the matter of baptism should not be encouraged. Except in very special circumstances the scriptural order is not to be upset (Acts 2.41-42). It is surely obvious that one who himself has not obeyed the Lord by being baptized is hardly qualified to instruct others in respect of Christian duties.

DISRUPTION. Fellowship in the assembly is

1. Disrupted by sin. As already stated on pages 36-37, fellowship with the Lord is hindered by a defiled conscience. When an offence involves others it must be brought to light, then judged and dealt with according to the procedure taught in God's Word. See page 71.

2. Disturbed by friction. Unhappily there are many causes of this and they are often petty and mean. One that sows discord is called in Scripture a worthless person, and if that discord be sown among brethren (or sisters) the disturber of harmony is strongly disapproved of God (Prov 6.12,14,16,19). Contrast Philippians 4.5 where moderation (gentleness, yieldingness, a sweet reasonableness that does not stand upon rights) is enjoined.

CHAPTER SIX

GOVERNMENT - OVERSEERSHIP

INTRODUCTION. It has been pointed out in an earlier chapter, that in Christendom church order as appointed by the Lord has been largely supplanted by human organization, especially in the sphere of rule and ministry. Traditions gathered from the writings of Greek and Latin Fathers, rather than the New Testament Scriptures, are appealed to in justification or condemnation of church doctrine and practice. Gatherings of believers endeavouring to follow the simple scriptural pattern are often charged with disowning leadership altogether, because no official class is in evidence among them. Without duly accredited leadership, however, an assembly would soon be in confusion like any community without government; cp. Judges 21.25. Christ is the sole Head of His Body the Church, and the Holy Spirit is His sole "Vicar" (co-equal in the Godhead) on earth. A visible "head" may appear to make a smoothly-running system, but it is God's order not man's arrangement that is to be our true guide. Recognition of Christ's Lordship necessarily involves a humble submission to any rule He may establish. Incidentally it is important to remember that brethren who bear responsibility of leadership are not to legislate but to administrate only.

The Lord has set up two forms of leadership in His Church, namely overseers ("bishops") and ministers ("deacons"). The former guide the local assembly, the latter serve it. "Governments" are to be distinguished from other "gifts", that is, administration must not be confused with ministry, though they are intimately connected (1 Cor 12.28). Note the order of address at Philippians 1.1: "saints" first, followed by "bishops" (overseers - plural) and "deacons" (ministering brethren).

DESIGNATION. The terms "overseers" (bishops) and "elders" (presbyters) refer to the same persons. The latter points to their age (i.e. spiritual maturity), the former to their work (Acts 20.17 with v.28; Tit 1.5 with v.7). Not all aged men are elders in the above sense (Tit 2.2-3 - Gk. word slightly different); cp. Job 32.9. Eldership goes back to Old Testament times and was continued among Jews in the synagogues (Ex 3.16; 24.1; Num 11.16, 24-25). In the early days the churches followed a similar simple arrangement of gatherings led by elders. Ritualists, however, have sought to model their services upon the more complex pattern of the temple worship. Elders are first mentioned in connexion with the church at Jerusalem and as collaborators with the apostles (Acts 11.30; 15).

COMMISSION. It is the Holy Spirit who sets overseers in the local church (Acts 20.28). He is the Divine Agent on earth of Christ the Head in heaven. God's Word knows nothing of the appointment of elders by ecclesiastical authorities, of election by congregations, or by existing elders. At first newly planted churches functioned without elders. Missionaries, who under God had been instrumental in gathering converts into recognized churches, on a subsequent visit chose for them certain brethren in the midst having spiritual and moral qualifications indicating to experienced eyes fitness for eldership (Acts 14.23). In a similar manner Paul instructed Titus to appoint elders in the churches in Crete (Tit 1.5). This in no wise gives countenance to the idea of apostolic succession, for the appointment conveyed no qualification to preach or to teach. Such ministry is after another order as we shall see later. We conclude that the procedure was inaugural and not intended to be continued once these assemblies were provided for. The writer believes we have here divine guidance for evangelists and missionaries in new spheres. Although the New Testament appears to give no specific directions for subsequent procedure, the principle of expediency enunciated by the apostle in 1 Corinthians would surely suggest that existing elders as spiritual guides should ever be on the watch for brethren possessing the requisite qualifications and indicate them to the assembly. They would then join the others in their prayers and consultations.

The appointment of a "bishop" with a "see" was an early departure from the New Testament order. The present system of ordination and nomination to the office with the granting of "livings" by the government, by some college or corporation, or even by unregenerate landowners, is certainly not of God but of the world.

FUNCTION. Eldership is strictly a local charge. It does not carry authority to rule in another assembly. Elders are not a board of officials set *over* an assembly but are labourers *among* the saints (Acts 20.28; 1 Pet 5.1-2; cp. Lk 22.24-26; Mt 20.25-28). The word "governments" does not precede but follows "helps" in the order of local grace-gifts (*charisma* - 1 Cor 12.28). It is omitted altogether in reference to the universal church (Eph 4.11). Whilst in general it may be desirable that they who attend to the business affairs of the assembly should be elder brethren, this work partakes of a "deaconing" nature, for which see next chapter.

In the Word of God the work of elders is described as

1. Shepherding (*poimaino*). Christ Himself is Chief Shepherd of His flock (1 Pet 5.4; Jn 10.16), and the elders are under-shepherds (1 Pet 5.2; Acts 20.28), in which passages "feed" means "to tend as a shepherd". Peter cites himself as an example (1 Pet 5.1; cp. Jn 21.15-17). Paul and Peter were not only apostles but pastors (i.e. shepherds) and teachers whose work ranged over the whole church (Eph 4.11). Today whilst there are no apostles in the primary sense, there are "sent ones" doing the work of shepherds and teachers in a wider sphere than one local assembly. "Pastor" (shepherd) indicates occupation with souls, "teacher" occupation with the Scriptures. The work of the former lies chiefly in private visitation, the latter's in public instruction. Incidentally both the apostles named were also evangelists, and Paul in particular a pioneer missionary.

The shepherd's duties, then, are to supervise, tend and feed the flock. Among the saints it is needful to instruct the ignorant, visit the sick, comfort the dying, console the bereaved, admonish the disorderly, encourage the faint-hearted, support the weak and restore the fallen, being long-suffering toward all (Jas 5.14; 1 Thess 5.14; Gal 6.1). Acts 20.34-35 indicates affording material help when necessary, either from one's own pocket or from assembly funds by arrangement. A true shepherd always pays particular attention to the lambs. It is interesting to notice that in His commands to Peter (Jn 21) our Lord uses a term which means to feed, or provide pasture for, the lambs (v.15) and growing sheep (v.17, best texts), but in v.16 a term which means to tend, covering the whole requirements of sheep in general. False shepherds are more concerned about shearing the sheep than about serving them. Hirelings are actuated by the pay not by love, so are not prepared to take personal risks (Jn 10.12-13). They feed themselves (Jude v.12; cp. Ezek 34.2-6). Sad to say many such are found in Christendom today! Teaching for hire came in with clerisy, under which system money often settles the sphere of ministry and determines doctrines to be taught or to be suppressed (Rev 2.6; Jude v.11; 2 Pet 2.15; Hab 1.15-16). Another has said, "Pastors *in* assemblies are invaluable; pastors *of* churches are unscriptural".

2. **Watching** (*agrupneo*) in the interests of souls (Heb 13.17). This is frequently linked with prayer, as in Ephesians 6.18. Adversaries are powerful, practised and persistent (1 Pet 5.8; Acts 20.29-31; Jn 10.12; 2 Cor 11.13-15; Mt 7.15-20). It is the work of shepherds to guard as well as to guide the flock (1 Sam 17.34-36). Laggards and stragglers among the sheep are in danger of being attacked by their foes. This is true also of the sick and feeble (Deut 25.18). The spiritual application is obvious.

3. **Leading** (*proistemi*, lit. to stand before; 1 Thess 5.12 - "are over"; 1 Tim 5.17 - "rule"). This is to be done with diligence (Rom 12.8). Eastern shepherds do not drive the sheep but lead them.

4. **Governing** (*hegeomai*, to rule, to preside, Heb 13.7,17,24). Elders are not to rule as "lords" (1 Pet 5.3; Mk 10.42-45). They are to be patterns not princes! A governor's authority is delegated not dictatorial.

5. **Steering** (*kubernetes* means a steersman, Acts 27.11; Rev 18.17). In 1 Corinthians 12.28 a cognate word is used metaphorically of "governments". Elders act as pilots in an assembly, steering it clear of dangerous "rocks" which might wreck its testimony.

6. **Labouring** (*kopiao*, to toil). This indicates wearying work as in Luke 5.5. Such is the task of the elders (1 Thess 5.12; 1 Tim 5.17; Acts 20.35). The little word "so" in the last passage points to Paul's manual work mentioned in the previous verse. An elder does not simply attend "brethren's meetings" to discuss assembly affairs, but toils among the saints for their spiritual good (Titus 1.9; Jude vv.22-23, RV), doing so always in a spirit of humility (1 Pet 5.5, RV).

7. **Stewarding** (*oikonomos* means a house steward, Lk 12.42). It is used metaphorically of a church elder ("bishop"). The Lord has entrusted elders with a responsible charge in His household, and in due time they must render account (Heb 13.17).

From the above it will be seen that the duties of elders are primarily connected with the spiritual welfare of the assembly, and only secondarily, if at all, with purely material things. These brethren should act in fullest fellowship with the rest of the saints. Mutual confidence is essential. If anyone should feel there has been some unjust exercise of rule on the part of the overseers appeal can always be made in prayer to higher authority, namely the Chief Shepherd and Head of the Church. Meetings of the oversight should follow the scriptural pattern (Acts 15.6; 21.18). The very plurality of elders suggests need to come together for prayer and consideration of assembly affairs. Unity of judgment is to be aimed at, for a divided oversight may lead to a divided assembly. Experience and expediency both suggest the undesirability of discussing every matter before the whole assembly with younger persons present. Questions can sometimes arise concerning the moral character of someone in fellowship and calling for possible discipline. Considerable harm is known to have been caused to innocent parties by giving to such matters wider publicity than necessary, especially when upon investigation allegations were found to be untrue. The elders are surely the proper ones to look into the case and afterwards advise the assembly without reporting all details. They are to take heed to themselves first of all, then to all the flock (Acts 20.28).

QUALIFICATION. Read 1 Timothy 3.1-7; Titus 1.5-9. Natural ability or business acumen, financial prosperity or social position neither qualify nor disqualify a brother for overseership. He must possess moral qualities as well as spiritual capacity for the work, a man of the Word, a man of faith, a man of prayer. In short he is to be sound in doctrine and conformed in life (Heb 13.7; 2 Tim 2.2). In ritualistic churches the personal character of an office-holder is not always taken into account. In private life a "priest" may be dissolute yet in virtue of his office he is permitted to "administer the sacraments" and even "pronounce absolution". In true Christianity it is far otherwise, as the above passages reveal. Eighteen words are used to indicate the character required in an overseer. Two phrases describe his capabilities and three his circumstances.

1. **Circumstances.** He must not be a novice, that is, a recent convert to the faith (1 Tim 3.6); note the reason and cp. 5.22. He is to be husband of one wife (1 Tim 3.2; Tit 1.6). This requirement would appear to indicate that in a land where plurality of wives is a legal custom, such a convert may be received into the assembly but is debarred from eldership. It would also take in the case of a divorced brother whose former wife or wives are still living. Such cases were by no means uncommon in the apostle's day owing to the corrupt facility of divorce allowed under Roman and Greek law. See W.J. Conybeare, M.A. in *The Epistles of Paul*. The elder must also possess a good testimony in the world (1 Tim 3.7). One discredited in business, for instance, would be disqualified; note the reason given.

2. **Capabilities.** An overseer is to be one who has his own household in effective control (1 Tim 3.4; Tit 1.6), again noting the obvious reason. He should be "apt to teach" (in Greek one word, 1 Tim 3.2); that is, not necessarily what is sometimes called

"a platform man", but he should be one able to impart instruction, privately at least, to younger believers.

3. **Character.** We cannot fail to note the high standard to be applied and followed. Summarized, we may say that besides the general principles already mentioned, an elder is to be irreproachable in conduct, sane and impartial in judgment, self-controlled in speech and action, reasonable in attitude (not stubborn or self-willed), free from avarice and disposed to hospitality.

RECOGNITION. Elders are recognized by the believers because they possess the requisite qualifications and do the work. Seven exhortations are found:

1. **"Know them"** (1 Thess 5.12). These words mean to know by observation. The Greek verb is never used of *formal* recognition. Knowledge leading to a more open acknowledgement is signified by another word found at 1 Corinthians 16.18 with v.16. Elders will obtain such recognition if they serve the saints well. Christ's sheep will instinctively follow without appeal or coercion one they have come to know and have learned to trust.

2. **"Esteem them"** (1 Thess 5.13). Saints are to value highly and appreciate in love these brethren on account of their work rather than from mere personal liking.

3. **"Honour them"** (1 Tim 5.17). Here "double honour" means that in addition to paying due respect material support should be afforded when necessary, as in the case of some who devote their full time to the work (v.18; cp. 1 Cor 9.7b). Paul's own example given at Acts 20.34-35, however, should not be disregarded.

4. **"Trust them"** (1 Tim 5.19 with v.1). No accusation is to be accepted against an elder except on the testimony of two or three witnesses, a principle based upon the Mosaic code (Deut 19.15). Elders are exposed to misrepresentation by very reason of their work, in advising the assembly in matters of discipline, for instance. If there be ground for remonstrance, deference as to a father is to be shown; yet if sin be proved there must be public reproof (1 Tim 5.20). Fellow-elders are not to condone or cloak failure in one of their number.

5. **"Obey them"** (Heb 13.17) refers to express injunctions. "Be submissive" refers to known but unexpressed wishes (1 Pet 5.5 RV; 1 Cor 16.15-16). Loyalty to leaders is enjoined because of their grave responsibility before the Lord.

6. **"Remember them"** (Heb 13.7) is urged in regard to leaders who had passed on, particularly perhaps to those who have suffered martyrdom. Saints are to consider the issue of their life, i.e. its triumphant finish, and to imitate their faithful example. The next verse reminds us that leaders may pass away but Christ ever remains as the one great Object of faith and service. Under-shepherds fall asleep but the Great Shepherd remains to raise up others, Himself exercising chief supervision of the flock (v.20; cp. 1 Pet 2.25).

7. **"Salute them"** (Heb 13.24). Greet them with kindly wishes that they may be encouraged in their work. They meet plenty of criticism! If the believers do not always agree with their decisions resentment should not be harboured. Pray for them (v.18; cp. 1 Thess 5.25; 2 Thess 3.1).

COMPENSATION. What a wonderful promise is found at 1 Peter 5.4, a promise to be fulfilled in the day of accounting (Heb 13.17; cp. 1 Thess 5.25; 2 Thess 3.1). This will surely be ample reward for the arduous and often thankless task of a true overseer!

CHAPTER SEVEN

MINISTRY - DEACONSHIP

DEFINITION. As used in the Scriptures, ministry denotes any form of service rendered to the Lord or to others. Examination of all passages where the Greek word *diakonia* and its cognates occur, immediately confirms this meaning. "Deacon" is a transliteration and simply means "servant". The service performed may be temporary or permanent. *Diakonos* points to the servant's relationship with his work. *Doulos,* another word often used, signifies a bond-servant, and it points to the servant's relationship to his master. In the New Testament *diakonos* may refer to a domestic servant (Jn 2.5-9), or a civil ruler as a servant of the State (Rom 13.4). It is used of Christ as Servant of Jehovah (Rom 15.8) and of Paul, Apollos and Timothy as servants of the Lord (2 Cor 3.6; 6.4; 1 Cor 3.5 and 1 Thess 3.2). There were also younger men who served the Apostle Paul and other leaders (Acts 19.22; Col 4.7; Philem v.13; etc). There were those who performed service *(diakonia)* on behalf of a local church (Acts 6.1ff; 11.29-30 with 12.25; 1 Tim 3.8-12), including a Christian sister (Rom 16.1). Even Satan has his ministers (lit. deacons, 2 Cor 11.14-15). A related verb is used of angels (Mk 1.13); of women (Mk 1.31; 15.41; Lk 8.3); and of Christ (Mk 10.45; Lk 22.27). The examination suggested should convince any unbiased person that *diakonos* does not indicate a title-bearing clerical official. Therefore, the commonly held view of a Christian "minister" as being one who holds the leading office in a church, following special theological training and ordination at the hands of superior clerics, perhaps receiving a stipend, is a grave misconception. The idea of one "minister" or "pastor" of a church is wholly foreign to Scripture teaching. 1 Timothy 3.10-13 in both AV and RV exhibits glaring examples of mistranslation in the interests of already established practices. "Office-of-a-deacon" represents a form of one Greek word meaning simply "to serve". Similarly "office-of-a-bishop" (v.1) represents one word only signifying "overseership". The use of the word translated "deacons" in Philippians 1.1 shows that these "servants" were a well-recognized group in the church at Philippi, being those who are sometimes called "ministering brethren".

COMMISSION. The current ecclesiastical practice of "ordination" to service is a clear usurpation of God's prerogative and of the authority of Christ, the Church's risen Head. It also presumes upon the function of the Holy Spirit (1 Cor 12.28; Eph 4.11; 1 Cor 12.7-11). Paul gives directions to Titus regarding the choice of elders, but nowhere in the New Testament do we find directions for the appointment of ministers in an ecclesiastical sense.

Servants are appointed directly by their own master (1 Pet 4.11). It is obvious that natural gifts cannot be bestowed by ordination of men. The same is true of spiritual gifts. Natural ability may be turned into spiritual channels by the grace of God but in itself it is no qualification for Christian ministry. Education is not the criterion of fitness for ministry, neither is it a bar thereto. Peter and John were not illiterate men (Acts 4.13). The Jewish leaders perceived that the two had not been trained in the recognized theological schools of the day. Saul of Tarsus had exceptional ability, theological training and high attainments (Acts 22.3; Phil 3.4-6). Nevertheless, before his conversion he held the mistaken notion that he was serving God, when, in fact, he was acting in violent opposition to Him (Acts 23.1; 26.9; 1 Tim 1.13). There are religious leaders in our time, who are equally misguided. The source of spiritual gifts is the risen Christ, who endows (Eph 4.11-12) and the power for their exercise is the Holy Spirit who endues (1 Cor 12.4-11; Lk 24.49; Acts 1.8). All mere fleshly activity in the things of God is wholly unacceptable to Him.

FUNCTION. In the Church two forms of ministry are discernible. First, there is service according to the spiritual gifts (*charismata* - grace-gifts), bestowed by the Head of the Church. Then there is service which has to do with temporal matters and material interests of believers. Both forms of service are distinguished in Acts 6.2-4: ministry of the Word and ministry of "tables".

1. **Service in the spiritual sphere.** Four main passages should be studied, namely Ephesians 4.7-16 for the universal church aspect; 1 Corinthians 14.4-31 for the local church aspect; and Romans 12.3-13 with 1 Peter 4.7-11 for the personal aspect. In the first passage our Lord is seen as an illustrious conqueror returning from a successful campaign against foes and proclaiming the great victory by a distribution of bounty. Christ's gifts are men appointed for the welfare and enriching of His Church. Four major grace-gifts are mentioned. Two were to pass as they belonged in a special way to the commencing period of the Church. Two have remained as permanent gifts for the whole of the church age. Apostles and prophets both possessed unique authority and miraculous powers as men through whom the Lord revealed New Testament truth, the former by personal teaching (Jn 14.26; 16.13-14; Gal 1.11-12), the latter by direct inspirational means (1 Cor 14.30). The apostles had seen the Lord (1 Cor 9.1; Acts 1.21-22), and had been specially chosen to be witnesses to His resurrection (Acts 3.15; 5.32; 10.41). Prophets communicated the mind of the Lord by an afflatus of the Holy Spirit. With the completion of the New Testament Scriptures which fully reveal the will of the Lord for His people, the need for these two great gifts passed. The permanent gifts are *evangelists,* whose proper sphere is in the outside world, though in intimate fellowship with the church, and *pastors and teachers* (a double gift in one person), whose sphere is within the church. The evangelist concentrates on preaching the gospel in order to win souls for Christ, planting new assemblies or bringing converts into association with existing ones. He is concerned with the church's expansion. The pastor (shepherd) and teacher concentrates on caring for the

saints, shepherding pointing to his occupation with souls, teaching to his occupation with the Word of God. As a shepherd his work is mostly in private, as teacher his work is more public. He is concerned in the church's consolidation. The change of terms used by Peter in his second Epistle (2.1) indicates that the prophets would be replaced by teachers. Both communicated the mind of God, but the former did so, as we have already seen, by direct revelation whereas the latter get their messages from the Scriptures. As with the prophet (1 Cor 14.3) so the teacher, too, is to speak to edification. Edification builds up, exhortation stirs up and consolation binds up (1 Cor 14.26). His ministry is constructive not destructive, a point sometimes forgotten by platform speakers.

1 Corinthians 12 enumerates grace-gifts in the local assembly and it is significant that "evangelist" is here omitted for, as we have stated, his work properly lies outside the immediate circle of believers though in full fellowship with them. Here, too, passing and permanent gifts must be differentiated. Prophecies, tongues and knowledge ("word of knowledge", v.8, i.e. knowledge derived from spiritual insight apart from direct revelation) were of this temporary character (1 Cor 13.8-10). Note that in Ephesians 4 the sign gifts are entirely omitted. A most important truth emphasized in 1 Corinthians 12 is that every individual believer shares the Christian ministry as a member of the Body of Christ. Not a single member of our physical bodies is without a function, and no believer is without some gift to be exercised to the upbuilding of the assembly (vv.12-27; 1 Thess 5.11; Rom 15.14). Christian sisters have their proper sphere in ministry (service); see the final chapter of this book, where the subject is examined. Some persons may possess more than one grace-gift. Another point that needs mention is that the major grace-gifts are not in sole possession of brethren who are in what is termed "full-time service". Brethren who follow a secular calling are often well equipped for ministry of the Word. The call to full-time ministry comes with distinct guidance from God and must not be taken up lightly (1 Cor 7.20; Mk 13.34).

All divinely-appointed ministry is primarily for the glory of God through Jesus Christ (1 Pet 4.10-11). The main purpose of the major gifts is to prepare and to fit all members of the Body of Christ for the exercise of their various functions with a view to the balanced development of the whole up to full growth and maturity (Eph 4.11-16, RV). Ministry, too, is a stewardship (1 Pet 4.10; 1 Cor 4.1 -2; 9.7). It looks to the day of accounting at the Bema of Christ. Diligence, love, patience and prayerfulness are among the many qualities enjoined upon all servants of Christ (Rom 12.3ff; 1 Pet 4.7-11). Gift is not to be neglected or laid up (1 Tim 4.14). At times it needs to be stirred up, rekindled as a fire (2 Tim 1.6). A true servant does not seek popularity but God's good pleasure (Gal 1.10; 1 Cor 7.23; Mt 6.1ff). The approval of the Lord is far better than the applause of men.

2. **Service in the material sphere.** An assembly may choose anyone to perform a service he or she may be willing and competent to undertake. Compare, for instance, Acts 6.1-6, where almoners were chosen in connexion with the distribution of daily rations to needy widows in the church at Jerusalem. These brethren were already approved servants of the Lord. They are not termed "deacons" *(diakonoi)* but their service is referred to in the passage by cognate words. Some of the chosen seven, if not all, were able to minister in a higher capacity. Philip is known to have been an evangelist (Acts 21.8). Compare his activities related in Acts 8.5-8 and 26-40. See, too, what is stated of Stephen in Acts 6.6,8,10. Other examples of "deacon-service" are found at 2 Corinthians 8.18-24 and at Romans 16.1. It is evidently a divinely established rule that if an assembly contributes funds for various purposes, its members should have a voice in the selection of brethren who administer or distribute the money or gifts in kind.

QUALIFICATION. The divine requirements are set forth in 1 Timothy 3.8-13. There are four positive and three negative - seven in all. Again, as in the case of overseers we note that a high standard is set; cp. Acts 6.3 where only temporal things are in view. Whether we take *gunaikas* in 1 Timothy 3.11 to refer to their wives (AV) or to women (RV) who serve the assembly, it is understandable that the four qualities mentioned should be required. "Faithful in all things" would appear to favour the RV translation, "things" pointing to matters entrusted to sisters by the assembly. On the other hand, the occurrence of the words in the middle of a list of instructions concerning deacons seems to favour the AV, but in that case why are similar injunctions not given in regard to the wives of elders? Able expositors appear to be about equally divided on the question. The present writer thinks it would not be wrong to apply the words to both classes of Christian sisters. Service and spirituality should go hand-in-hand (2 Cor 6.3-10; 1 Thess 2. 1-12).

REGULATION. For notes on the regulation of ministry in the principal gatherings of the assembly see Chapter 3 herein. Others have pointed out that a brother may have a gift suited to a small local company consisting mostly of immature believers, but not gift that would profit, say, a united ministry meeting of Christians drawn from a wide area and of all stages of spiritual growth. Much distress is sometimes caused by some who have no proper gift for public ministry yet who persist in taking the platform only to weary the saints with profitless talk. Such behaviour wastes both time and money expended in arranging such gatherings. In flagrant cases of offence the procedure advocated in Titus 1.10 should be adopted.

RECOGNITION. Those who claim the call of God to ministry are to be tested as to soundness in doctrine, consistency in life, and capability in service. If proved "blameless" (that is, give no ground for complaint) they are to be permitted the liberty of serving among the saints according to their proper grace-gift (1 Tim 3.10; Mt 7.15-20). The assembly is thus responsible to recognize and to provide room for those whom God has set in the midst (1 Cor 16.15-18). It must not be forgotten that an assembly can neither appoint nor control any grace-gift, and certainly should not hire or retain solely for its own benefit any servant of Christ. Even an apostle had no authority to direct a fellow-servant of the Lord (1 Cor 16.12). Moreover, a servant of Christ is not to be judged as to service, sphere and motive, for he serves in view of the Bema (Rom 14.4, 10; 1 Cor 3.5-15; 4.1-5).

Elders, as responsible leaders in an assembly, should ever be on the look-out for signs of gift in younger men and encourage such by affording opportunity for exercise and development towards maturity (2 Tim 2.2). There appears to be need in these days to stress the importance of Paul's injunction to Timothy, for this will ensure a true "apostolic succession" in the Church of God.

The Master supplies the needs of His servants (Lk 22.35). His promises are all-sufficient to assure one who has been charged by Him with ministry. Nevertheless, where necessary, practical recognition by rendering financial support is enjoined upon the saints: see 1 Corinthians 9.7, 13-14; 3 John vv.5-8 (evangelists); Galatians 6.6 (teachers); 1 Timothy 5.17-18 (elders who labour in the Word). In this last passage, as pointed out in a previous chapter, "double-honour" means paying them due respect and in addition granting them a suitable honorarium. Paul's example in special circumstances and for valid reasons should not be overlooked by the Lord's servants (Acts 20.33-35; 1 Cor 9.18; 2 Cor 11.7-12).

COMPENSATION. For faithful service the Lord has graciously promised abundant recompense (Mt 25.21-23). Moreover in the church a good standing is attained (1 Tim 3.13, RV). The criterion of judgment is not the measure of success but the degree of faithfulness (1 Cor 3.8; Rev 22.12).

CONCLUSION. "How can I recognize a gift in myself?", is sometimes asked. We may summarize in an alliterative way by way of answer; Fervour - Faculty - Fruit. First, is there *due ardour* for a particular line of service? Next, is there *definite ability* for that particular line of service? Lastly, is there *divine approval* upon that particular line of service? One should ask oneself, "Has the Lord blessed my service hitherto?", and, "Can I count upon the commendation of my brethren in this?". 1 Corinthians 12.31; 14.1 and 39 undoubtedly refer to the assembly but by implication may be applied to the individual Christian. "Greater" means greater usefulness, not necessarily greater prominence. No brother should seek a position he has no ability to fill. If he faithfully uses gift already possessed, the Lord may be pleased to add further gift.

CHAPTER EIGHT

DISCIPLINE

MEANING OF DISCIPLINE. The word "discipline" is not found in the AV but the idea is there under the term "chastening" (*paideia*, childtraining). In its wide sense it signifies training by instruction and correction, but in a narrow sense correction only is in view. Discipline of an individual or assembly and discipline by an assembly should be distinguished. The former is by direct action of the Lord and is His prerogative alone. The latter is His mediate action through an assembly whose solemn duty it is. The one has to do with order in the "family" of God, the sphere of relationship. The other with order in the "house" of God, the sphere of responsibility. The former is illustrated by 1 Corinthians 11.29-32, the latter by 1 Corinthians 5.1-13. Differentiate also between God's judgments inflicted in righteous anger upon the ungodly world and the chastening of His own children, which is a seal of sonship and proof of the Father's love (Heb 12.5-13; cp. Rev 3.19). Discipline by direct action of the Lord is commended to the reader as a most profitable study, but our lesson is concerned rather with discipline in and by an assembly. This matter is almost completely ignored in the sects of Christendom, though so clearly taught in God's Word. Discipline is the more necessary in these days because the lawless spirit of the age has forced itself into the churches through the worldliness and carnality of so many professing Christians. This lawless spirit characterized Israel in the days of the judges (Judg 21.25).

Three assembly responsibilities are to be noted, namely

(a) the reception of true believers; (b) the rejection of gross offenders; and (c) the restoration to fellowship of such as are truly repentant. The assembly must not shelve a question of discipline and leave the matter with the Lord simply because an unpleasant duty is involved (1 Cor 5.12-13). The church at Corinth was sharply reproved for lack of prompt action in a case of flagrant immorality in the midst. The believers had adopted an easy tolerance of the evil and were more concerned, even "puffed up", in the possession of many spiritual "gifts". Neglect in exercising discipline dishonours the Lord, hinders the work of the Holy Spirit, and mars the assembly's testimony. Mutual concern is to be shown on the principle of 1 Corinthians 12.25-26. Discipline, then, in the sense of our present lesson refers to methods adopted to deal with persons who upset godly order in an assembly.

OBJECT OF DISCIPLINE

1. **Negative aspect.** Discipline is not a trial of faith but of conduct; that is, it is not to decide whether a person is a believer or not (2 Tim 2.19). Neither is it a convenient way to get rid of a troublesome brother towards whom patience needs to be shown and prayer made to God for him.

2. **Positive aspect.** The exercise of discipline should always have in view the following aims. First, restoration of the offender (2 Cor 2.5-11; Gal 6.1); then, the maintenance of the assembly's integrity before God as a "temple" fit for His presence in the midst, and before men that all appearance of toleration of evil may be removed. Next, an instance of discipline furnishes a warning to all the saints lest a careless walk lead to similar lapses. Lastly, but not in order of importance, there is the necessity to vindicate the name of the Lord by the removal, as far as humanly possible, of the reproach brought upon it before the world. If not immediately dealt with evil spreads like leaven (1 Cor 5.6; Gal 5.9). Compare the law as to "leprous" stones in a house (Lev 14.40-41); also Joshua 7 where the sin of Achan is shown to have involved in its consequences the whole congregation of Israel.

CASES OF DISCIPLINE. Contrary to a notion commonly

prevailing, excommunication is not the only form of discipline. God's Word shows this is to be resorted to only as a last expedient. Seven categories of offence, some more serious than others, seem to be indicated as follows:

1. **The Personal Offender** (Mt 18.15-20; Lk 17.3-4). See also the NOTE on page 74.

(a) *Nature of Offence.* This is purely a matter between individuals. Evil-speaking or breach of trust may be cited as examples.

(b) *Method of Procedure.* Here is no question of excision. Three stages are enjoined. First, the delinquent is to be shown his fault. If he repents, implying apology, and amends, he is to be forgiven. Note the measure of patience to be exercised (Mt 18.21-22, 35; Lk 17.4; Eph 4.32; Col 3.13). The second stage is still of a private nature (Mt 18.16). After the third stage (Mt 18.17) if efforts prove unsuccessful, the offender is to be treated by the wronged one ("unto thee" - not the whole assembly) as an outsider. Until the matter is straightened out there can be no fellowship between the two. Matthew 5.22-24 is from the viewpoint of one who knows he has given real cause for complaint.

2. **The Overtaken Brother** (Gal 6.1-3).

(a) *Nature of Offence.* A temporary lapse is contemplated, not the pursuing of an evil course. The brother is "pursued", so to speak, and overtaken by the temptation. He is tripped up at an unguarded moment.

(b) *Method of Procedure.* The Greek word translated "restore" primarily means to readjust. It is used also of reducing a dislocated joint, of mending broken nets (Mk 1.19, etc). 1 Timothy 5.20 although referring primarily to an elder conveys a general principle. The rule is, therefore, private offence, private rebuke - public offence, public rebuke.

3. **The Meddlesome Idler** (2 Thess 3.6-15; 1 Thess 4.11-12).

(a) *Nature of Offence.* It is one of walking disorderly, especially in disobedience to the Word (2 Thess 3.14). The Greek translated "disorderly" sometimes indicates "out of step", lack of co-ordination even to the point of insubordination. The form of disorderliness specified here is that of being a "busybody" (lit. one who "works around"), that is, who moves among the saints not for edification but for gossip, evil-speaking and "hanging-on" for some selfish interest.

(b) *Method of Procedure.* Such a person is to be warned by the elders (1 Thess 5.14). Should this prove unavailing, the saints are bidden to withdraw themselves (2 Thess 3.6,14). This is not the same as excommunicating but it is a curtailing of fellowship (v.15). Faithfully carried out this action should bring the offender to his senses.

4. **The Unprofitable Speaker** (Tit 1.9-14; 1 Cor 14.26, 29).

(a) *Nature of Offence.* The brother referred to is one who persistently wastes the time of the saints in profitless "ministry" (Tit 1.10; cp. Job 15.2-3).

(b) *Method of Procedure.* There is to be warning and sharp reproof (Tit 1.13) in order to silence such men (vv.10-11). Elders are responsible to prevent such abuse of liberty. Neglect of this step may lead to factions (Tit 3.9-11). In this passage "heretical" is not said of one who denies the faith, but of one who in self-will seeks to gather adherents to his opinions especially in matters of interpretation and other things not of vital importance. Such conduct is factious and may even end in open division; see next paragraph.

5. **The Division Maker** (Rom 16.17-20, RV; Tit 3.9-11; Acts 20.30).

(a) *Nature of Offence.* A serious evil is that of causing division among the saints and affording occasions of stumbling. Included are legalists and others who distort some element of truth and sway certain believers to such a degree that a party spirit is fostered even to the point of divisions. Differences in opinion or in judgment should never be allowed to lead to this state of things.

(b) *Method of Procedure.* In the first place reproof may be effective (Gal 2.11-14; 1 Tim 5.20). If this fails then according to the above Scriptures believers should "mark", "avoid", "turn away from" these persons. It is obvious that if this procedure is followed by all, divisions cannot occur. At Corinth, though the Christians were professedly one, there was imminent danger of division into rival parties (1 Cor 1.10-15). Such a state was evidence not of spirituality but of carnality. The devil is the instigator of this evil and the flesh is ever ready to respond (Rom 14.18 with 20). Ponder the double warning to elders and their double responsibility (Acts 20.28-31).

6. **The Gross Evil-doer** (1 Cor 5.1-13; 6.9-10).

(a) *Nature of Offence.* A person guilty of some grave moral lapse, such as listed in 1 Corinthians 5.11 is to be disciplined. "Fornicator" covers all cases of illicit sexual intercourse. "Covetous" covers all manifestations of evil desire for gain seen in various forms of gambling, sharp practice in business, etc.; cp. Ephesians 5.5; 2 Peter 2.14; 1 Timothy 6.9-10. The term "idolater" includes any active association with false systems of worship (though they may bear a Christian label), sorcery and spiritism. "Reviler" takes in one guilty of vilification or defamation of character or making false accusations, one who is given to such behaviour. "Drunkard" contemplates a person who has fallen into the habitual sin of intemperance rather than one coming under the category of the overtaken brother. "Extortioner" would include all open cases of dishonesty, such as misappropriation of property or funds, fraud and profiteering, especially in the necessities of the poor (Jas 5.1-6).

(b) *Method of Procedure.* This is clear. "Put away from among yourselves" signifies a formal rejection from assembly fellowship to be followed by complete severance of social relations (1 Cor 5.11-13). It is not simply a denial of the privilege of partaking of the Lord's Supper. Sometimes a careful investigation of the circumstances may be called for, but at Corinth there was open sin with facts well known, hence no inquiry was needed. Such a disciplinary measure throws the offender back into the sphere of the world where Satan rules and he becomes fully exposed to the devil's attacks (1 Cor 5.5; 1 Tim 1.20; 2 Tim 2.25-26). That the action taken by the church at Corinth was effective in bringing the guilty brother to repentance, so making restoration possible, is seen by reference to 2 Corinthians 2.1-11; 7.9-12.

7. **The Unsound Teacher** (2 Pet 2.1-3 RV; 2 Jn vv.9-11; 1 Tim 4.1; 2 Cor 11.13-15).

(a) *Nature of Offence.* The case is one of propagation of evil doctrine. Fundamental error is in question not mere differences of interpretation in non-essentials such as dispensational teaching. However, the latter like any over-stressed doctrine if unwatched may lead to heresy. Evil doctrine can be more destructive than loose morality, for common opinion is swift to denounce the latter among Christians, but gives little heed to the former.

(b) *Method of Procedure.* Assembly action is the same as in cases of moral evil. It is leaven which must be purged out (Gal 5.9; 1 Cor 5.6-7). The apostle deals similarly with both types of evil (1 Cor 5.5 with 2 Tim 2.18; 1 Tim 1.20). No social intercourse is to be permitted (2 Jn vv.9-11).

PRINCIPLES OF DISCIPLINE. The following are general considerations.

1. **Judicial fairness is always to be employed.** The Christian standard is higher than that of world courts (1 Cor 6.2-3). Godly order suggests careful investigation by elders, who should reject unsupported testimony (Mt 18.16; 1 Tim 5.19). The assembly may then be furnished with a brief report of essentials only. It is not the elders but the assembly that acts in "putting away" when necessary.

Partiality must be rigidly excluded (1 Tim 5.21; Jas 3.17; 2.1-4). Judgment is not to be influenced by natural relationship or friendship (Acts 15.36-39). Extremes are to be avoided. Undue severity may divide the assembly and undue lenience tends to increase the evil. Unbalanced action destroys the confidence of the saints in their leaders and dishonours the Lord, that is, harshness in minor matters while neglecting divine principles (Mt 15.1-20; 23.23-24; Lk 11.42; Rom 14.1-3; 15.7). Such lack of balance was found in Israel in the days of the Judges; see chs. 17-20. There was unanimous and violent reaction against a case of immorality, but laxity and indifference in a matter involving gross idolatry, a matter which brought grave dishonour upon the name of Jehovah.

2. **Scripture order is to be strictly observed.** The "cutting off" of an assembly or group of assemblies is quite unknown in God's Word. Notwithstanding the carnal condition of the church at Corinth it was not "cut off' by other churches. In Revelation 2-3 we find that the Lord has much to reprove in several of the churches but He gives not the slightest hint of any cutting off by the others. It is solely His prerogative to remove the "lampstand" if He sees fit (2.5; 3.16). Where serious moral or doctrinal evil continues to be tolerated in an assembly, godly ones may have to consider withdrawal from it as from a "disorderly" person, but only after all protests have proved unavailing and other measures fail. Hasty action is to be avoided and there should be much prayer exercise before taking this grave final step.

3. **Assembly decisions are to be loyally supported.** Misplaced sympathy with an offender only encourages him in his evildoing and so hinders repentance and restoration. It puts the sympathizer into the category of the "unruly" as partaker of the evil and makes him or her liable to discipline also (1 Tim 5.22; 2 Jn v.11). No believer under discipline in one assembly should be readily received in another. If after due inquiry by the elders the first assembly is adjudged to have been over hasty or too severe, it would be well to approach the elders of that assembly with a view to aiding reconciliation. To act otherwise would be subversive of godly order and might involve a breach of fellowship between the assemblies concerned.

4. **Offender's withdrawal is to be juridically ignored.** If an offender ceases to attend the meetings in order perhaps to avoid the disgrace of public rebuke, the assembly is not thereby absolved from taking action. However, it is essential to differentiate between absence through coldness of heart, which calls for shepherd care, and absence to escape discipline.

5. **Offender's repentance is to be sufficiently attested.** Restoration to the Lord precedes restoration to church fellowship. True repentance is evidenced by departure from the evil and the making of restitution when possible. Scripture does not advocate undue delay (2 Cor 2.5-11). Wise discernment is

needed coupled with brotherly love (1 Cor 13.4-8; Gal 6.2). The restored one would do well to refrain, for a time at least, from public service for God, to prove his sincerity by a humble spirit and a consistent walk. There is no definite rule as to this. Peter's restoration after his sad lapse was a matter of days only, but it must be remembered that our gracious Lord knew Peter's heart, whereas our knowledge of men is limited. Lack of commendation for some special service or disapproval of it (Acts 15.36ff) and disqualification for overseership (1 Tim 3.1-6) do not affect church fellowship.

NOTE:

Arising out of an unhappy situation existing in the locality where he is serving the Lord, a missionary reader asks what action, if any, should be taken if the offender still remains obdurate after the aforementioned procedure has been fully carried out yet both parties continue to attend and take part in the assembly gatherings ... Such a situation is not unknown (alas) elsewhere.

Assuming the offended one is observing the principle of Luke 17.3-4, it would then seem well for elders with full knowledge of the circumstances to remind the offender of Matthew 5.23-24 warning him that he is laying himself open to the charge of unruliness which is liable to discipline according to 1 Thessalonians 5.14-15 and 2 Thessalonians 3.6. This step has been known to prove effective. It falls short of action referred to in paragraphs 6 and 7 above. Meanwhile the rest of the assembly should be exercised in private and public prayer beseeching the Lord to heal the breach which mars the assembly's united witness for Him.

CHAPTER NINE

FINANCE

INTRODUCTION. The question of finance which so often presents anxious problems to the churches of Christendom, is really simple if the scriptural order is observed. Nowhere in the New Testament are we given the slightest hint that the world is to be appealed to for funds in carrying on the Lord's work. They who do so are dishonouring God. Giving to the Lord is a privilege belonging to His people, whose offerings alone, spiritual and material, are acceptable to Him. As to other men God appeals to them in the gospel to receive His free gifts not to give; cp. Romans 6.23, RV. It is particularly reprehensible to take up collections at gospel meetings, whether indoors or out. In sending out his preachers our Lord enjoined them, "Freely (i.e. gratuitously) ye received, freely give. Get you no gold, nor silver, nor brass (copper or bronze money) in your purses" (Mt 10.8-9, RV). Paul was careful to adopt this policy, labouring with his own hands rather than be chargeable to his hearers at Corinth (2 Cor 11.7-9; cp. Acts 18.3; 3 Jn v.7). It is true that he gives a special reason for this (2 Cor 11.12), a reason that God's servants would do well to take into consideration in similar circumstances. The salvation of God is obtained "without money and without price" (Is 55.1; cp. Eph 2.8-9). On the other hand, a common practice of announcing, "No collection", is inadvisable for gospel meetings. This sounds too much like advertising generosity and sensitive folk may feel it to be a reflection upon their pockets!

There will be abundant supply for all needs in the Lord's work if Christians recognize their privilege and rise to their responsibility in accordance with the precepts of God's Word. Importunate solicitation, burdensome exactions, worldly expedients and elaborate financial organization all will then be unnecessary. Such unworthy methods call down the just reproach of the world upon the Church as a money-making concern.

PROVISION OF FUNDS. It is a fundamental principle that all a believer has belongs to the Lord. He himself is not his own and all his possessions are held in trust as a steward of God (1 Cor 6.19-20; Rom 12.1; Lk 16.9-13; 2 Cor 8.5). Under the Mosaic economy God claimed back from the Israelites a certain portion of their possessions on a similar principle, namely, that all they had was first given to them by Him. He claimed the first-born males of man and beast, though the offspring of man or ass could be redeemed by a lamb as a substitutionary sacrifice (Ex 13.1-2, 11-15). The first-fruits of the land were His also (Ex 22.29-30). The tithe belonged to Him, and this He gave back to the tribe of Levi in lieu of a common share in the division of the land of Canaan among the tribes of Israel. Tithing was observed by Abraham before the giving of the Law (Gen 14.20; Heb 7.4-10). In Israel to withhold any part of the tithe was to rob God (Mal 3.8-10). In addition sacrifices and certain prescribed portions of sacrifices were the Lord's. All these were obligatory as a rendering up of that which did not properly belong to Israelites. Giving to God in the true sense began only after these requirements had been met. Of such a nature were the "free-will" offerings which, as this name indicates, were wholly voluntary. First mention of a voluntary offering by the Israelites is in connexion with a supply of materials and work for the tabernacle of Jehovah (Ex 35-36). Regarding sacrifices of a volitional character read Leviticus 22.17-25; 23.38; Deuteronomy 23.21-23; etc. These passages all contain instruction applicable to Christian giving. Further examples may be seen at the time the first and second temples were built (1 Chr 29; Ezra 1.4-6; 2.68-69).

Under grace the act of giving is wholly spontaneous but the standard should hardly be less than under the Law, even as the privileges Christians enjoy are far superior to those of Israelites. Five times in the New Testament giving is termed a "grace", being that which in the Christian is responsive to the revealed grace of God in salvation.

1. **Means of Giving.** As we have seen, these lie with each individual believer, and instructions are found chiefly in 1 Corinthians 16.1-3 and 2 Corinthians 8-9, which passages repay close study. In the former the expression "each one of you" should be noted. It embraces everyone in the assembly, though the well-to-do may have greater ability and wider opportunities (1 Tim 6.17-19). The churches of Macedonia gave out of their poverty (2 Cor 8.2-4), and the first principle in all giving is stated in v.5. Women disciples manifested this grace and the Lord accepted their ministry. Brethren wholly engaged in the Lord's work are not exempted from this duty. They are like the Levites of old, who both received tithes and gave tithes (Num 18.25-32).

2. **Measure of Giving.** Giving is to be according to each person's ability (2 Cor 8.11-12; Acts 11.29), and "as he may prosper" (1 Cor 16.2, RV). Liberty not law rules (2 Cor 9.5), but inasmuch as God is a liberal giver, His children should be like Him (Jas 1.5; Jn 3.16; Rom 8.32, etc). Our Lord impoverished Himself to make us rich (2 Cor 8.9). His superlative grace is an incentive to all (Rom 12.8, RV; 2 Cor 8.2; 9.11,13). Let us not forget the Lord's estimate of measure (Mk 12.41-44; Lk 21.1-4), or His promises (Lk 6.38; cp. 2 Cor 9.6; Prov 11.24-25; 22.9).

3. **Motive in Giving.** On the negative side it is not to be for the admiration of men (Mt 6.1-4), therefore our giving should be done without ostentation and, as far as may be possible, privately. The world's way is to publish lists of charitable gifts, placing the names of people who contribute the largest sums at the top! On the positive side the motive is love to God and to man (1 Cor 13.3; 2 Cor 8.8; 1 Jn 3.17-18; Gal 6.10). The constraining power of divine love not human appeals should actuate us. Furthermore we should give to the glory of God (1 Cor 10.31).

4. **Manner of Giving.** Scripture says "willingly" (2 Cor 8.3, 11-12) and "cheerfully, without grudging" (2 Cor 9.7; Acts 20.35).

If we are to provide things honest in the sight of all men we shall give only what is rightly ours (Rom 12.17; cp. RV). Debts to tradesmen, family obligations, etc. must not be overlooked (Rom 12.8; Mk 7.11-13; 1 Tim 5.8; 2 Cor 8.20-21). Also requisite is a clear conscience in relationship with our brethren if our gifts are to be acceptable to the Lord (Mt 5.23-24).

5. **Method of Giving.** God's Word teaches us to give systematically not haphazardly (1 Cor 16.1-2). This is done by laying up in store proportionately to income and purposefully as before the Lord. Many keep a special box at home for this. Well-to-do brethren sometimes have a separate banking account. Others simply make a book-keeping entry. It is from such a store that gifts are made whenever one is exercised by the Spirit of God. The embarrassment that may be caused by a sudden call is thereby avoided (2 Cor 9.5). This regular setting aside links the act with the worship and the remembrance feast of the Lord's Day. It is interesting to recall that in Israel this was the day of the presentation of firstfruits, both the wave sheaf and the wave loaves (Lev 23.9-21).

COLLECTION OF FUNDS. Joint giving is exemplified in Acts 11.29-30; Romans 15.25-26; 1 Corinthians 16.1; Philippians 4.15-16. Individual giving is indicated in 3 John vv.5-7; Galatians 6.6; Hebrews 13.16; 1 Timothy 6.18; Acts 4.36-37. Contributions for local church expenses can scarcely be regarded as giving to the Lord. Rent, furnishing, lighting and heating and care-taking, for instance, are all necessary to secure the comfort and convenience of the saints themselves. Sharing such expenses is surely a matter of duty, a debt rather than a "free-will offering".

ADMINISTRATION OF FUNDS. This should be in the hands of more than one brother (Acts 6.3-6; 1 Cor 16.3-4; 2 Cor 8.18-21; 9.3-5). It is a wise arrangement which leaves no room for unkind suspicions. It also increases the confidence of the saints and spreads the burden of responsibility. Although such brethren minister in temporal things, their moral and spiritual qualifications are to be high (Acts 6.3; 1 Tim 3.8-13). Obviously they must also possess a measure of capacity for business. From these and other passages of Scripture it would appear to be a divine principle that those who contribute the funds should have a voice in the selection of brethren to take charge thereof. Other than the possession of the requisite qualifications no indication is given of the method of choice. Elders as "guides" in the assembly, it would seem, are free to judge the most expedient way of discovering the mind of the saints. Accounts should be rendered to the assembly at regular intervals, again on the godly principle of 1 Corinthians 14.40; 2 Corinthians 8.20-21.

DISTRIBUTION OF FUNDS. In the New Testament we see four main avenues for disbursing the gifts of the saints, not forgetting what we have already written regarding local assembly expenses.

1. **Poor Saints** (Rom 12.13; 15.23-27; Gal 2.9-10; Acts 11.29-30; 24.17; 2.44-45; 1 Cor 16.1-3; 2 Cor 8 and 9; Prov 19.17). There is no lack of opportunity (Mk 14.7). The indolent and thriftless are not to be considered (2 Thess 3.10-11). Compare the charge to Israel (Deut 15.7-11).

2. **Needy Widows** (Acts 6.1-6; 1 Tim 5.4-16). Not all widows in the church qualify for this aid. They must be really destitute, having no relatives able to support them. They should be at least 60 years of age. They are to commend themselves as women of prayer and trust in God, and are to be bearers of a character approved for godly living and useful activity.

3. **God's Servants** (Phil 4.15-19). It is to be observed that this includes evangelists (1 Cor 9.4-14), teachers (Gal 6.6) and elders who give their full time to shepherding and teaching, if they have no private means of support (1 Tim 5.17-18). We have elsewhere urged that Paul's example should be copied when certain questions of expediency arise (Acts 18.3 with 20.34). Such a course might be advisable in places like Corinth in order to remove all suspicion of mercenary motives (2 Cor 11.7-12). However, at the same time the apostle did not refuse to accept gifts from other churches (vv.8-9). To the Ephesian church Paul afforded an example in Christian giving (Acts 20.33-35). In Thessalonica also he laboured to avoid burdening the saints, who were both poor and suffering persecution (1 Thess 2.9; 2 Thess 3.7-9).

4. **Philanthropic Efforts** (Gal 6.10; 1 Thess 5.15). The Christian is not prohibited from contributing to charitable funds for worthy objects but discrimination is needed. The household of faith has always a prior claim upon the help of God's people.

We may now mention the *results* of and the *rewards* for giving. Of the former seven are indicated, as follows: -

(a) It is well-pleasing to the Lord (1 Cor. 9.7; Heb 13.16; Phil 4.18).

(b) It brings relief to necessitous saints (2 Cor 9.12).

(c) It stimulates others to like effort (2 Cor 8.1-2; 9.2).

(d) It promotes thanksgiving in grateful recipients (2 Cor 9.11-14).

(e) It evokes prayer for the kind-hearted givers (2 Cor 9.14).

(f) It increases ability for further giving (2 Cor 9.8-10; Prov 11.24; Lk 19.24-26). Here are both principle and promise.

(g) It produces fruit to swell the donor's account (Phil 4.17; 2 Cor 9.10).

Besides the rewards seen in the above there is joy in doing the will of the Lord and in assisting those in need. There are also precious promises such as in Proverbs 11.24-25; Luke 6.38. The Lord has been pleased to point to further approval in a coming day. Faithful stewardship ranks high in His gracious estimation (Mt 6.19-21; 25.24-30; Lk 16.9-13; 19.11-26; 2 Cor 9.6). We should bear in mind also the principle enunciated by Christ (Mt 25.40; 10.42). A "well done" from Him is assured as well as a "well come" (welcome) from many friends in the eternal tabernacles (Lk 16.9).

There is one matter that needs, perhaps, to be brought forward at this point. It is hardly becoming in servants of the Lord to advertise personal needs. Paul and the other apostles did not do so, although they did make known the needs of distressed saints. Information is frequently desirable but solicitation is not. Servants of Christ look to their Master alone for support. He it is who moves the hearts of His people in right directions to meet the requirements of His servants. Gifts for personal use should be acknowledged, of course, either by word or by letter and an account of stewardship rendered for the disbursement of entrusted funds.

CHAPTER TEN

DEVELOPMENT AND DESTINY

DEVELOPMENT. Attention is first drawn to a distinction of great importance, namely, that between the Church and Christendom. As we saw in Chapter 1, the former is composed solely of born-anew persons. The latter is the mass of religious profession bearing the name of Christ. The Kingdom and the Church are to be differentiated also. In Scripture these terms are not synonymous. Failure to observe this distinction has led many astray into false interpretations and grievous doctrinal errors. The Church is included in the Kingdom but is not co-extensive with it. The Church was inaugurated at Pentecost and will be completed at the Translation, often termed the Rapture. The Kingdom overlaps in time. It has three phases or periods. The *ministry phase* began with the preaching of John Baptist (Mt 3.2) and the presence of the King (Mt 4.17). It ended with the rejection of the King by the Jews (Mt 12), which they confirmed by a later declaration (Jn 19.15). The *mystery phase* then began (Mt 13.11), its history being given by our Lord in parabolic form, and carries on through the present age up to the return of the King in glory. It is this phase that corresponds so nearly with Christendom, the progress of which is instructively set forth in Matthew 13.24-33. The *manifestation phase* will begin when the King returns to inaugurate His personal reign on earth. This period is commonly known as the millennium (thousand years, Rev 20.1-10). The kingdom was long foretold by prophets of old, but the Church was a mystery (secret), which from all ages was hidden in the counsels of God until the appointed time of its revealing (Eph 3.3-11; Col 1.24-29).

The development of the true Church is in two ways, external and internal, better expressed, perhaps, as from without and from within. All is basically the work of the Holy Spirit. Development from without is mainly by the agency of evangelists, but all believers are to share the work of evangelical witness. This is the growth towards *entirety* described under the figure of a building (see Chapter 1). Development from within is mainly by the agency of shepherds and teachers, but it is also accomplished by the proper functioning of every believer according to the grace-gift bestowed by the Lord. This is growth towards *maturity,* described under the figure of a body (refer again to Chapter 1). The former development is progress by expansion, the latter progress by consolidation.

Progress by Evangelism. The universality of Christ's saviour-hood is revealed by passages such as Luke 2.29-32; 3.6; John 4.42; Romans 1.5; 1 Timothy 2.6-7. In accord with these is the Lord's comprehensive commission (Mt 28.18-20 and Mk 16.15; Lk 24.47). The divine plan calls upon all believers to be witnesses, as the scope of these Scriptures and Acts 1.8 indicates. A witness is one who tells what he has personally seen and heard, what he himself has experienced and therefore knows. The immediate band of early disciples were specially chosen to be witnesses to the facts of Christ's death and resurrection (Acts 1.22; 2.32; 3.15; 4.33; 5.32; 10.39-41; 13.30-31). To these facts Paul also could witness (22.14-15; 26.16-18; 1 Cor 9.1). Believers are witnesses in a more general sense, luminaries in this dark world, holding forth the word of life (Phil 2.15-16). Local churches are witnesses in their corporate capacity. This is revealed in the Apostle John's vision of the seven lampstands (Rev 1.12,20). Three essentials to church witness are shown in the Philippian Epistle, 1.27-28. They are (a) *consistency* - a worthy behaviour; (b) *cooperation* - a united effort; and (c) *courage* - a fearless attitude. Life and lip must be in accord. The church at Thessalonica bore such a testimony, a witness to the world and an example to other saints (1 Thess 1.6-10).

It is a great mistake to look upon evangelizing as the sole responsibility of gifted evangelists. In the Acts record "evangelizing" is predicated of men and women believers, who were scattered abroad owing to persecution at Jerusalem (8.4). The word translated "preaching" here is *euangelizo*. In 11.20 the same word occurs and is there associated as in the previous verse with an informal telling out of the gospel. The chief words translated "preach" are (a) *euangelizo*, which means to announce glad tidings, and this points to the nature of the message; (b) *kerusso*, to proclaim as a herald, pointing to the authority of the message; and (c) *kataggello* to proclaim, which has an intensive force as setting down the truth before the hearers.

It is important to bear in mind the purpose of God in this present age. It is not the conversion of the world as so many imagine, but is stated in Acts 15.14 to be visiting the Gentiles to take out of them a people for His name. It is the out-calling of the church of Christ, and the challenge of Romans 10.14-15 is insistent in this connexion. Very noticeable is it that in Scripture no provision is made for elaborate organization and the need of it is not contemplated; cp. Acts 5.42. We have so often seen in our lessons that simplicity is the keynote of divine order in relation to church activities. Through the testimony of the early disciples, there was progress by addition and multiplication (Acts 2.41-47; 5.14; 6.1,7; 9.31; 11.24).

The *evangelist* is not merely a preacher of the Word but one specially gifted by Christ to be a winner of souls. He concentrates on proclaiming the gospel, planting new churches or bringing converts into existing ones (1 Cor 3.5-9). He does not establish "groups" or "circles". The true evangelist should have a zeal for the Lord, a passion for souls and a clear understanding of the gospel. While identified with a local assembly and commended by it (Acts 13.3), he goes out into the world with the word of reconciliation (2 Cor 5.18-20). He is ready like Philip to preach to crowds or to a single individual, to visit a busy city or to follow a desert track (Acts 8). Philip is the only person in Scripture actually called an evangelist (Acts 21.8), but Paul was certainly one (Rom 1.15; 15.18-21) and Timothy may be safely included (2 Tim 4.5).

The evangelist's great objective is to bring men into right relationship with God by conviction, confession and conversion. His primary aim is to glorify God. His true power comes from the Holy Spirit. The medium through which the Spirit operates is the Word of God (1 Pet 1.23-25). The apostles preached "the word", "Jesus and the resurrection", "the kingdom of God", "Christ and Him crucified", "the gospel" (glad tidings). They presented clearly in simple fashion the facts of Christ's death and resurrection with the reasons therefor, aptly summed up by Paul (1 Cor 15.3-4). Much of today's preaching is not of this character. Within the limits imposed by scriptural principles, ways of presenting the gospel may be adapted to changing times and conditions. Our eyes cannot be closed to the sad fact that in Christian home-lands the weekly gospel meeting as we know it fails to meet present needs. Gospel Halls as well as denominational churches are largely shunned by unsaved people, yet many seem to be firmly wedded to the traditional order of meetings, forgetting that God's Word affords no such rigid pattern. The Lord's messengers in apostolic days followed the Master's command to "go" rather than expect people to "come" to them. In the Book of Acts we find them visiting private homes as well as public buildings, Jewish synagogues as well as Greek market-places. They preached by roadside and riverside, in schools and in lodgings, in prisons and in palaces, in short, wherever they could obtain a hearing for the glad tidings. It is significant that our Lord used the illustration of fishing to describe evangelistic work. It was a subject with which His Galilean disciples were not only familiar but in which some of them were experts (Mk 1.16-20; Lk 5.1-11). Line fishing and net fishing both have their application to methods of evangelism. A successful fisherman has to study closely the habits of the fish, times and seasons and suitable bait to use. Above all he must go to the place where the fish are!

Much might be said, and needs to be said, concerning modern methods of evangelism, especially some mass "revivals" in which popular preachers introduce undesirable features appealing to people's love of novelty and excitement. True servants of God should ever be on their guard against copying worldly tactics so derogatory to the dignity and solemnity of the gospel message. So-called "decisions" are not necessarily conversions, yet this frequently appears to be the aim in many mass campaigns. There is urgent need to return to the more simple methods of apostolic days.

Another procedure that has grown up in recent years, if not

fully approved, seems to be countenanced by Christians among whom one would least expect to find departure from New Testament principles. One refers to the practice of certain preachers, who spend most of their time moving about among well-established assemblies to preach the gospel, when all the while there are large areas where there is little or no testimony for God and where multitudes are ignorant of the gospel. It is possible they are not wholly to blame. They are encouraged by brethren who find it much easier in these days of life's increased pressure to put hand in pocket for the support of such ministry rather than give time for waiting upon God in prayer and study of His Word in a desire to fill the need in the local gathering. Timothy was admonished not to neglect the gift that was in him (1 Tim 4.14). Another possible cause of the procedure just mentioned is that some assemblies who readily extend practical fellowship to missionaries in foreign lands often forget financial help to "home-workers" labouring in the neglected districts of a city or in remoter areas of their own land, unless these workers pay a personal visit to report on their labours. Assemblies should ever be ready to foster local gift by affording room for its exercise. A properly functioning church will be provided by the Lord with ample grace-gifts for its needs. Should there appear to be a lack, it is quite proper to desire and to pray for the bestowal of greater gifts (1 Cor 12.31).

Missionary Work. The word "missionary" does not occur in our English Bible but the concept is there. The missionary is one who has a mission from God and he usually possesses the gift of evangelist, but not necessarily so, for his mission may be to teach or do other work for the Lord. Our word comes from the Latin form of the Greek word for apostle, meaning one who is sent. The corresponding verb is commonly used in the New Testament for sending on a mission of any sort, without reference at all to the special band known as apostles. "Missionary" is now usually applied to one who goes to an unevangelized country with the gospel. Though the word is convenient to use it does tend to create an artificial distinction between the Lord's servants labouring in the homelands and those occupied in distant lands. The field is the world (Mt 13.38) and each labourer has his own proper gift and sphere in service for the Master. Nevertheless, it is well that all God's people should cultivate a world view of Christian witness and not hold to the insular, constricted, local view that is all too common (Jn 4.35; Mt 9.37-38). Questions concerning the individual's call to service, his commendation, conduct, control and communication, lie outside the scope of our present study, but they are of great importance.

Progress by Edification. Growth of the Church by the edification (building up) of itself in love is the subject of Ephesians 4.1-16 and Colossians 2.19 (the universal aspect); 1 Corinthians 12-14 (the local aspect). To effect this there is a Spirit-set overseership and a God-ordained ministry (refer to Chapters 6 & 7 herein). Ephesians 4.11-13 should be read in the RV and it will be understood that the major grace-gifts are to be exercised with a view to the perfecting of the saints unto the work of service. This means that all believers as members of the Body of Christ are thus to be equipped and encouraged to fulfil the function proper to each for the growth of the Body until full maturity of the whole is reached.

DESTINY. In the divine plan the Church subserves God's purpose for the glory of Christ (Eph 1.9-10, 22-23). Her visible unity is not designed for the present age because she is not yet complete, although as a distinct entity she had pre-existence in the eternal counsels of the Godhead (Eph 1.4; 3.1-13). Her visible association with the Head awaits the day of Christ's manifested glory. However, unity should be exhibited among believers even now, so far as may be consistent with loyalty to the Word of God (Eph 4.3; Jn 17.21-23). The Church conceived in eternity and created in time is now the vehicle for the display of God's wisdom to the higher intelligences (Eph 3.10; cp. 1 Cor 11.10). At the same time she is the means of testimony for God to men as a light in the world's darkness (Rev 1-3). Ultimately she is to be the vehicle for the display of God's grace (Eph 1.6; 2.7) and for the display of God's glory (Eph 1.12, 14; 3.21; cp. 2 Thess 1.10).

Regarding the Church's eternal destiny comparatively few details are revealed, doubtless for the reason that our poor finite understanding would utterly fail to grasp the glories of it. The very cost to the Lord of her redemption assures us of the infinite blessedness of her future portion. What the Word of God does make known, however, is sufficient to sustain the hearts of the saints amid the trials of the present scene, and to encourage faithful witness and zealous service. The proper hope of the Church is to be forever with her Lord, and this will be consummated at His personal descent to the air (1 Thess 4.17) according to His promise (Jn 14.3) and to His desire (Jn 17.24). She is to be His companion in millennial and eternal glory (Rom 8.17-18, 21, RV; Rev 19.7; 21.9; 22.5).

The Order of Events connected with the Lord's coming is set forth below. It should be understood that the word translated "coming" in these Scriptures is *parousia*, which means "presence" and is so rendered in the RV margin. It is a word which in the New Testament denotes a period rather than an act. This may be clearly seen by its use in Philippians 2.12 where it is set in contrast to a period of *apousia* (absence). Compare our use of the English word "coming" in the sense of a visit, indicating not merely the act of arriving but an undefined period during which many events may take place and many projects carried out. The period of Christ's "presence" begins with His descent to the air (1 Thess 4.15-17) and ends with the manifestation (*epiphaneia*, a shining forth) of His presence at His advent in glory (2 Thess 2.8).

Events having to do directly with the Church are:-

1. *Resurrection of the sleeping saints* (1 Thess 4.16).

2. *Transformation of the living saints* (1 Cor 15.52; Phil 3.20-21).

3. *Translation of the whole company* (1 Thess 4.17). The Old Testament saints share this blessed experience although they form no part of the Church, for they too belong to Christ (1 Cor 15.23; Heb 11.40).

4. *Examination at the "Bema" of Christ* (1 Cor 4.4-5; 2 Cor 5.10; 1 Cor 3.13-15; Rom 14.10). This will be a review of the life and will result in reward for service. It decides future dignity not future destiny.

5. *Presentation to the glorified Christ* (Eph 5.25-27; Jude vv.24-25). Compare the type in Eve (Gen 2.22-23). It should be noted that the final adjustments made at the Bema are an essential preparation for this.

6. *Celebration of the Lamb's marriage* (Rev 19.6-9; Eph 5.32). A

"secret" which is then fully revealed is the relationship which Christ has established between Himself and His Church. Heaven is the Church's true sphere. As the Body of Christ, she is *nearest* to Him of all the families in heaven and in earth that derive their being from God, and as the Bride of Christ she is *dearest* to Him (Eph 5.25). A double preparation for her proper home is to be observed. Divine grace has fitted her for it (Col 1.12) and personal conformity has exercised her (Rev 19.8, RV). Divine righteousness belongs to the church by gift (Rom 3.21-22). Personal righteousness (lit. righteousnesses) is hers by deeds (Rev 19.8, RV). Christ's Bride prepares part of her own trousseau!

7. *Manifestation with Christ at His appearing* (Col 3.4; Rom 8.19-23; 2 Thess 1.10). This is the public exhibition to the world of the true relationship between Christ and His church. Having shared His reproach and rejection on earth she is seen then to share His reign as Son of Man in the millennial kingdom (2 Tim 2.12).

Events Subsequent to the Appearing. The church's further destiny is:

1. *Millennial Glory,* in which she is associated as consort with Christ in universal rule (Rev 20.4-6). Here we see vision (v.4), parenthesis (v.5a), and interpretation (vv.5b-6). Compare Acts 17.31; 1 Corinthians 6.2; Revelation 2.26-27; 5.10 ("on the earth" is better rendered "over the earth"). The Church is both a recipient and a reflector of divine glory, presenting unfading beauty and shedding inconceivable brightness over the millennial scene (Rev 21.11, 23-24, RVm).

2. *Eternal Glory,* in which the Church still appears in eternal youth and bridal splendour unchanged after one thousand years. Revelation 21.2 shows her in the eternal state and vv.9ff in the millennial state. Regarding the eternal state one should study closely not only Revelation 21.1-8 but also 1 Corinthians 15.24-28; Ephesians 3.21 and 2 Peter 3.13. The glory of heaven for all believers may be summed up in four terse phrases, namely: *See Him* (1 Jn 3.2); *With Him* (1 Thess 4.17; Jn 14.3; 17.24); *Like Him* (1 Jn 3.2); *Serve Him* (Rev 22.3).

CHAPTER ELEVEN

THE SPHERE AND SERVICE OF WOMEN

To gather the mind of God on this subject it is well to consider, first of all, woman's origin.

CREATION ORDER (Gen 1.27-28; 2.18-25). In His eternal counsels God ever had before Him the glory of His beloved Son. This included provision of a consort wholly suited by grace to be for ever in joyful fellowship with Him as the Christ, a fit vehicle for the display of divine wisdom in time and divine grace in eternity (Eph 3.10-11; 2.7). God's order in creation is to be viewed in the light of this planned union of Christ and the Church (Eph 3.10-11; 5.32a; Col 1.26-27). In relation to God she was "created" (Gen 1.27); in relation to man she was "made" (lit. builded) from his side (Gen 2.22). When considered in its context v.20 is of profound import. God took evident delight in His creature-man's exercise of divinely bestowed wisdom in naming beast and bird, but there was a deeper purpose in the act. It was clearly demonstrated that Adam's being was of an entirely different order and that among all other creatures that passed before him there was no true counterpart "answering" to him. The words "was not found" suggest an unsuccessful quest. It would seem that the Creator in gracious consultation with Adam, showed him that a suited consort could come only from his own body. The implication is that man's willing response as a free agent was to offer himself for the operation necessary to produce his bride. Not only is greater force thus added to vv.23-24, but it answers more closely to the wonderful antitype of Christ and the Church (Eph 5.25-32). It is surely evident that God never intended the woman to be in the place of independence. Her position, however, is not one of inferiority but of unique dignity as representing the Church's relationship to Christ, a dignity to be worthily sustained according to the divine arrangement; cp. Proverbs 31.10-31. Without the woman man is incomplete and the divine purpose for him frustrated (1 Cor 11.3). The whole context of this verse to v.12 repays careful study.

The Fall did not alter the relative position of man and woman but the effects upon the latter are stated in Genesis 3.16. These were suffering in childbirth and subjection to her husband. Headship had been vested in the man before, but now subjection on the part of the woman was a matter of command rather than of a spontaneous attitude. Modern teaching and practice have largely nullified God's order, resulting in much of the confusion to be observed in present-day society (1 Cor 11.3).

Matrimony is according to the Creator's arrangement (Gen 2.24), and was endorsed by our Lord (Mt 19.3-6; Jn 2.1-2); compare Hebrews 13.4 and the implied rebuke against forbidding it (1 Tim 4.3). Divorce was never intended by God, and modern practice in regard to this is another cause of the deplorable state into which society has drifted in these days. Scripture teaching on the subject will be found in Matthew 5.31-32; 19.7-12; Mark 10.2-12; Luke 16.18; Romans 7.1-3; 1 Corinthians 7 and elsewhere. During periods of special distress such as open persecution of the Church of God, it may be expedient for the time being to refrain from or postpone marriage in order to minimize dangers and difficulties (1 Cor 7.26-31). Then there are cases in which servants of the Lord will suffer less distraction by remaining free from family ties as, for example, those doing pioneer missionary work in more or less unexplored territories (1 Cor 7.32-35; Mt 19.12). The apostle Paul was probably such a one (1 Cor 9.5 with 7.8). Marriage involves definite commitments and the New Testament by giving precepts and recording examples instructs in the respective duties of husband and wife (1 Cor 7; Eph 5.22-23; Col 3.18-19; 1 Pet 3.1-7). In proper subjection to her husband the Christian woman should be an example to the world instead of an imitator of it.

The Home is woman's special sphere of activity. 1 Timothy 5.14 speaks of her as the "houseruler". This does not mean, of course, that she is head of the family. Her aim is to make the house into a home, and this can be done only where love prevails. She is to be "husband-lover" and "children-lover" (so the Greek), discreet, chaste, good (that is, "beautiful" in character though she may not possess good looks) and a "home-worker" (Tit 2.4-5). Income is mostly the husband's earnings but much of the responsibility for expenditure devolves upon the wife, who, as another has said, ". . . has to decide between necessities and luxuries with conveniences in a middle place!" The training of children, especially in their younger years, lies chiefly with the mother. This is a great privilege and a solemn duty on no account to be neglected. Lack of well-ordered homes is, perhaps, the greatest cause of juvenile delinquency so prevalent today.

Adornment. The fall of man wrought a change from the primeval condition (Gen 2.25). The attempt of the guilty pair to cover their sin and shame proved a complete failure (Gen 3.7-8). They themselves realized this immediately they heard the voice of God, which betokened His presence in the garden. The wronged Creator in sorrowing love provided for their recognized need by the death of substitutionary victims (Gen 3.21). In the light of subsequent procedure there is little reason to doubt that under divine direction man the sinner did the blood-shedding (Gen 3.21). In this way the truth afterwards stated in Leviticus 17.11 and Hebrews 9.22 was brought home to the consciences of Adam and Eve in a forcible manner. We see a clear fore-shadowing of the redemptive work of Christ. The wearing of clothes, even the scanty covering of uncivilized tribes, bears striking testimony to the fact of the Fall. Animals have no such self-consciousness. The cult of nudity is but one of man's many efforts to deny the Fall by removing evidence! The Law enjoined a distinction between the attire of men and of women (Deut 22.5). The words in the latter part of this verse imply that God intended it to be an abiding principle. Christian women are instructed to wear apparel that is seemly with modesty and discretion. Neither immodest nor slovenly dress commends the gospel. There is to be no ostentation or extravagance. The believer should be approved by good deeds not by glamorous dress, by consistent works not by costly wrappings (1 Tim 2.9-10). God looks upon the heart not on the outward appearance (1 Sam 16.7). This should encourage sisters who do not possess beauty of features and form. A meek and quiet spirit is precious in God's sight and should be highly esteemed among Christians. Men and women of the world may be attracted by the artificial styles of fashion, but these are corruptible and soon pass away (1 Pet 3.3-4; 1 Jn 2.15-17; Rom 12.2). Certain adjustments necessary for health and comfort in various climates are not ruled out, but conspicuousness is to be avoided whether in new fashions or old.

With respect to so-called "beauty-aids", the only woman named in the Bible who used them is Jezebel, Ahab's wicked wife, surely an unenviable character for Christian sisters to follow (2 Kings 9.30). In the writings of the prophets we read scathing denunciations of the use of make-up, though applied to God's people, perhaps, in a metaphorical sense also (Jer 4.30; Ezek 23.40). As to the hair, it was designed of God to mark a distinction between the sexes (1 Cor 11.14-15a). Long hair is woman's glory, therefore some modern practices which surrender to passing fashion cannot be well-pleasing to the Lord (1 Cor 10.31). Trimming for health reasons may be advisable on occasion provided this is done with a clear conscience before God and not offered simply in excuse. A woman is to be truly feminine and not to ape masculinity. Both nature and revelation reprehend a woman with shorn head (1 Cor 11.6,15). Many present-day fashions and practices are really a sign of revolt against the Creator's decrees.

REDEMPTION ORDER. In this there is no distinction of sex (Gal 3.28). All believers are alike in Christ Jesus, in Christ a new creation (2 Cor 5.17). All are partakers of the heavenly calling (Heb 3.1), and all have equal share in the privileges of the Christian priesthood (1 Pet 2.5,9). This blessed standing before God must not be confounded, however, with the present church order.

CHURCH ORDER is to maintain a testimony for God before angels and before men (1 Cor 11.10; Eph 3.10-11; 1 Cor 14.23-25). In the Christian assembly the creation order still holds (1 Cor 14.34-35; 1 Tim 2.11-15). In the latter passage reasons for this are given, namely (a) a man's priority in creation (cp. 1 Cor 11.2, 8-9); (b) woman's frailty in transgression; (c) woman's fidelity to function. It is noticeable that when tempted by Satan Eve acted wrongly in independence of Adam. Moreover, fulfilment of her function is properly and mostly in the family sphere not in a public capacity. Therefore, in all assembly gatherings and among mixed audiences leadership is invested in the men. This refers to both teaching and audible praying (1 Tim 2.8,12); "the men (lit. adult males) ... in every place" (RV) is surely a clear enough statement. No restrictions appear to be placed upon sisters speaking and praying in gatherings for women or children, provided the injunction as to a head-covering is observed in accordance with 1 Corinthians 11.2-16. Many women have natural ability for speaking but neither this nor modern practice in certain churches warrants disobedience to the Word of God, however plausible arguments may sound. Apparent blessing upon such efforts is no true guide (Mt 7.21-23; 2 Cor 5.9). We need ever to be on guard lest the spirit of the age (Eph 2.2) should encroach upon the Lord's territory. Satan is always working to subvert the divine order, but his defeat is assured and his doom certain and imminent (Rom 16.20).

The ministry of Christian women has scope in a wide sphere of activities for which they are particularly suited. As a member of the Body of Christ, each has her function to perform for the edification of the whole (1 Cor 12.7,12ff). Most wives and mothers will find their time chiefly occupied in home duties. A well-ordered Christian household is a powerful witness for God in any neighbourhood. Elderly women, widows and unmarried sisters may have more opportunity to engage in outside work such as teaching a Sunday School class, visiting the sick and sorrowing, distributing tracts, helping the singing in open-air witnessing, taking part in gatherings of women, and in personal work among neighbours. Elderly sisters are enjoined to teach the younger (Tit 2.3-4). Again, we have an example of a Christian wife sharing with her husband in the enlightenment of a brother not so well instructed in the way of God (Acts 18.26). Wives of elders in particular may be able to render valuable assistance in undertaking investigations among womenfolk on behalf of the assembly, and perform other services, provided always that they possess the requisite qualifications similar to those given in 1 Timothy 3.11; cp. Titus 2.3. In the showing of hospitality to servants of Christ and other visiting saints, also to lonely believers, especially younger ones from ungodly homes, the wife obviously has the greater share (1 Tim 3.2; 5.10; Tit 1.8; Rom 12.13; Heb 13.2; 1 Pet 4.9; cp. Acts 16.15,40). Christian women in the medical profession, nurses and school teachers all have an exceptional field to witness and work for the Lord. Examples of other forms of service are found in Matthew 27.55; Mark 12.41-44; 15.41; Luke 8.3; Romans 16.1; Acts 9.36-39. In practice women have often proved most generous givers. The Word of God records many examples of women who displayed strong faith and rendered devoted service to God. Among the list of "honourable mentions" in Hebrews 11, we find named and unnamed women. A host of dear sisters in Christ, little noticed in the world, will meet in a coming day the approving word of their Lord, "She hath done what she could" (Mk 14.8).

MISUNDERSTOOD TEXTS. It would appear well to consider some of the passages advanced in support of public ministry by Christian women, Scriptures referred to by those who wish to introduce this mistaken practice into assemblies.

(a) *1 Corinthians 14.34-35.* The prohibition found here is alleged to refer to chattering in assembly gatherings. The Greek verb used occurs frequently in the New Testament but never in the sense of "to chatter". In this very chapter it appears twenty-four times, twenty-two times clearly relating to ministry. Let the reader attempt to substitute the word "chatter" in any of these occurrences and he will immediately perceive the resulting absurdity. Take v.29 for example! Besides, would not the chattering of men be equally reprehensible? Why place such a restriction upon the sisters only?

(b) *Acts 21.9-10*. This passage mentions, not without significance, that the four daughters of Philip the evangelist possessed the prophetic gift. There are no true prophets now so that in any case no example is afforded for the present day. In modern times the only women claiming the prophetic gift have been connected mostly with error cults, like Mrs. Baker Eddy of "Christian Science", Mrs. Ellen White of "Seventh Day Adventism" and not a few others. We are not told that Philip's daughters exercised the prophetic gift in public. Moreover, we cannot fail to observe that when a prophetic message concerning Paul was to be delivered, the Lord sent His servant Agabus all the way from Judaea instead of using Philip's daughters who were already on the spot. No support for the public ministry of women can be found here.

(c) *Philippians 4.2-3*. Euodias and Syntyche laboured with Paul in the gospel, but it is an unwarrantable assumption to suggest that they preached in public or even preached at all. As we have seen, there are many ways in which Christian sisters can co-operate in the Lord's work apart altogether from speaking.

(d) *John 4.28-30,42*. In considering this Scripture three things are to be noted. First, the Samaritan woman's audience was composed of "the men", that is, those with whom she was acquainted and had had in all probability unholy relations. Next, hers was a simple testimony not a public address (v.39). Thirdly, she issued an invitation, no doubt individually, saying "Come, see . . .". This work of inviting people is an admirable form of service for Christian sisters.

(e) *Acts 1.14*. It is not to be inferred that the women prayed audibly. The order of the words both in the Greek and in the English indicates simply that the women were present. Had the statement been, "These all, with the women, continued steadfastly in prayer" there would be a measure of ambiguity. As it is, the meaning is clear.

(f) *Judges 4.4-9*. Advocates of women's public ministry must be hard put to it when they turn to such an Old Testament passage. There is no inconsistency, however, even here, but rather a warning example. Rulers had ceased in Israel (5.7), showing that all was in confusion in the nation instead of divine order. Deborah took over responsibilities for the civil rule for lack of a man able and willing to do it. Barak was a military leader but so weak and fearful that when an emergency arose he called upon Deborah to share the post of danger with him despite her warning (4.9). The incident shows utter weakness and failure among God's people at that time. There was certainly not "an accession of new power and spirituality", which is advanced as a plea by some who would permit Christian women to have full liberty for the exercise of a "speaking" ministry. Such brethren expose in themselves Barak-like defects and augment sad failure so manifest in the churches today. Hebrews 11.32 mentions Barak's name but omits Deborah's, thus upholding the divine principle that where men and women are in association even in weakness, leadership properly belongs to the men.